The Dupe Hunter - A Field Guide to Eco-Friendly and Sustainable Travel

Experience 5-Star Luxury, Escape the Crowds, Discover Hidden Gems, and Slash Your Footprint While Supporting Locals

Sienna Wilder

Contents

Dedication 1

Introduction: The Manifesto of the Dupe Hunter 3

- Let's start with a horror story.
- The Problem: We Are Loving the World to Death
- The Solution: The Art of the Dupe
- The Promise: Progress, Not Perfection
- How This Book Works

Chapter 1: The Hunter's Mindset: Why "Perfect" is the Enemy of "Good" 8

- This is the Guilt Trap
- The "Imperfect" Advocate
- The Tale of the Failed Eco-Trip
- The 3 Rules of the Hunt
- Workbook Element: The "Traveler vs. Tourist" Self-Audit

Chapter 2: The Search Engine Strategy: Hacking the System 14

- The Tool: The "Map View" Supremacy
- The Algorithm: Visual Hacking
- Section: Timing the Market
- Action Steps: Setting the Trap
- Conclusion: The Blank Slate

Chapter 3: The "Eco-Lodge" or The "Eco-Lie"? Detecting Greenwashing 20

The Great Towel Scam
The "Ick": Performative Sustainability
The Greenwashing Detection Kit
The Certification Jungle
Red Flags vs. Green Flags

The "Greenwashing" Betrayal 27

Chapter 4: The European Swap: Champagne Vibes on a Beer Budget 31
Part I: The Canal Conundrum
Part II: The Mountain Meltdown
Part III: The Island Illusion
Part IV: The Logistics: Tagskryt (Train Bragging)
Part V: The Breakdown

Chapter 5: The Tropical Swap: Paradise Without the Plastic 42
Part I: The "Eat, Pray, Loathe" Complex
Part II: The "Eco-Chic" Charade
Part III: The "Disneyfication" of Nature
Part IV: The Reef-Safe Reality

Chapter 6: The "Rawdog" Rebellion: Silent Travel & Digital Detox 53
Part I: The Flight of the Rawdog
Part II: Silence is the New Luxury
Part III: The Destinations
Part IV: The Digital Boundary
Part V: Workbook Element: The Sensory Log

The "Vipassana" Panic Attack 65

Chapter 7: Train Bragging (Tagskryt): Making the Journey the Flex 69
Part I: The Mindset Shift
Part II: 5 Epic Rail Journeys

Part III: The Night Train Renaissance
Part IV: The Man in Seat 61
Part V: The Social Flex
The Night Train Confessional 79
Chapter 8: The "Slowmad" Protocol: Depth Over Breadth 83
Part I: The Mathematics of Stasis
Part II: The "One Base" Rule
Part III: Community Integration
Part IV: The Ethical Minefield
Part V: The Narrative Arc of a Slowmad Month
Part VI: The "Slowmad" Toolkit
Part VII: Case Studies
The "Third Place" Breakthrough 95
Chapter 9: Feast Like a Local: Avoiding the "Tourist Menu" Markup 99
Part I: The Anatomy of a Trap
Part II: The "Menu Del Dia" Strategy
Part III: The Market Hack
Part IV: The Zero-Kilometer Diet
Part V: Street Food Safety
Part VI: The Alcohol Strategy
Part VII: How to Order (When You Don't Speak the Lingo)
Part VIII: The Narrative: The Best Meal of My Life
Part IX: The "Feast Like a Local" Checklist
Chapter 10: The Ethical Gear Guide: Aesthetic Minimalism 114
Part I: The Philosophy of the Carry-On
Part II: The Fabric Revolution
Part III: The "Eco-Gear" That Actually Looks Good
Part IV: The Toiletries Revolution
Part V: The Water Strategy

Part VI: The Tech Setup
Part VII: The Bag Itself
Part VIII: The "One-Bag" Packing List Checklist
Part IX: Laundry: The Hobo Bath for Clothes
Part X: The "Buy It For Life" (BIFL) Mindset
Chapter 11: Wildlife & Welfare: Don't Be That Person 130
Part I: The Disneyfication of Nature
Part II: The Golden Rule
Part III: The "Sanctuary" Scam
Part IV: The Dupe Strategy
Part V: The New Rules of Engagement
Part VI: The Narrative: The Bear in the Berries
Part VII: The Welfare Check
Part VIII: The Redemption
Chapter 12: The Return: Reintegration & Redemption 143
This is the Post-Travel Blues
Part I: The Hangover
Part II: The Carbon Ledger
Part III: Redemption
Part IV: Digital Altruism
Part V: The Legacy of the Hunter
Conclusion: The Manifesto of the Dupe Hunter 152

Dedication

Writing a book about travel is a paradox. You spend months locked in a room, staring at a screen, trying to describe what it feels like to be outside. It is a lonely, neurotic, indoor process dedicated to the art of being somewhere else.

This book has my name on the cover, but it belongs to the people who actually did the work.

First, to the Gatekeepers.

To the grandmother in the Mekong Delta who grilled me a prawn on a rusty brazier and didn't charge me the "tourist price." To the guesthouse owner in Theth, Albania, who kept the fire going when the power went out. To the barista in Lisbon who didn't roll his eyes when I ordered coffee in broken Portuguese for the thirtieth morning in a row.

You are the ones keeping the soul of these places alive while the rest of the world tries to pave them. Thank you for letting me in, and thank you for feeding me.

To the Fixers and the Rangers.

To the people patrolling the Virunga mountains in the rain to keep the gorillas safe. To the scientists replanting coral in water that is getting too hot. To Mark Smith (The Man in Seat 61), whose obsession with train schedules has saved more carbon than any government policy. You are the adults in the room. I'm just the one taking notes.

To my Editors and Early Readers.

Thank you for telling me when I sounded like a preachy, self-righteous jerk. Thank you for cutting the chapters where I ranted for ten pages about plastic straws. Thank you for reminding me that nobody wants to read a lecture; they want to read a story. You saved this book from my own worst impulses.

To my Family.

For tolerating the "Rawdog" experiments. For listening to me talk about "carbon insetting" at the dinner table until your eyes glazed over. For understanding that when I said, "I need to go to Mexico for research," it wasn't a vacation... it was work. (Okay, it was a little bit of a vacation. But I appreciate you letting me get away with it).

To the Disasters.

To the missed trains, the leaky hostel roofs, the food poisoning, and the rainstorms that ruined the "perfect" view. You taught me that the best travel stories are usually the ones where everything goes wrong. You taught me resilience. You prevented this book from being a polished, Instagram-perfect lie.

And finally, to You.

The person holding this book.

You could have bought the "Top 10" guide. You could have booked the all-inclusive cruise and turned your brain off.

But you didn't. You chose the hard way. You chose to hunt.

Thank you for giving a damn. Thank you for caring about where your money goes and what your footprint looks like.

The world is fragile, but it is still beautiful. Thanks for helping to keep it that way.

Now, put the book down. Go outside.

The train is leaving.

Introduction: The Manifesto of the Dupe Hunter

Let's start with a horror story.

It's 11:30 AM on a Tuesday in July. You are standing on the edge of the Caldera in Oia, Santorini. This is it. The moment. The desktop background you've been staring at since February. You are supposed to be having a spiritual awakening while gazing at the Aegean Sea.

But you aren't having a spiritual awakening. You are having a panic attack.

You are currently wedged between a sweaty honeymooner from Wisconsin and a frantic influencer with a ring light who has elbowed you in the ribs twice in the last three minutes. The famous blue domes are barely visible behind a wall of outstretched iPhones. The air doesn't smell like sea salt and oregano; it smells like diesel fumes from the tour buses idling below and the distinct, anxious body odor of three thousand people realizing they made a terrible mistake.

You are thirsty, but the nearest café has a line out the door and is charging €15 for a lukewarm soda. You want to leave, but you can't, because the narrow, whitewashed alleyways are gridlocked with cruise ship passengers who have just been disgorged onto the island like krill into a whale's mouth.

You feel scammed. You feel exhausted. And worst of all, you feel guilty, because you spent six months savings and two tons of carbon to get here, and all you want to do is go back to your hotel room and doom-scroll.

Welcome to the "Santorini Scaries". This is what happens when we love a place to death.

Now, let's rewind the tape. Let's change the coordinates.

Same time. Same Tuesday in July. But this time, you are on the island of Paros, just a short ferry ride away.

You are sitting at a wobbly wooden table under a bougainvillea tree that looks like it's been there since the Odyssey. It is quiet. Not the eerie silence of an empty room, but the rich, living silence of the Mediterranean wind moving through olive groves. There is no line. There is no ring light.

An old man named Kostas puts a carafe of chilled white wine and a plate of grilled octopus on your table. The octopus was in the ocean this morning. The wine costs €3. You can hear the waves lapping against the rocks, and when you look up, you see the exact same Aegean blue, but without the filter of five hundred other people's heads.

You feel smug. You feel relaxed. You feel like you got away with something.

This is the "Paros Peace"[4]. And this book is about how to find it, over and over again.

The Problem: We Are Loving the World to Death

Look, I'm not here to tell you that you're a bad person for wanting to see the Eiffel Tower or swim in Bali. We all have that itch. We are hardwired to explore. But we have to be honest about the fact that modern tourism has become a monster that is eating its own tail.

We say we love travel, but what we're actually doing is engaging in a frantic, extractive scavenger hunt. We treat the world like a backdrop for our content rather than a place where actual people live. We descend on the same ten "Must-See" locations, drive up the prices until the locals can't afford to live there, erode the coastlines, and turn vibrant communities into hollowed-out theme parks.

It is expensive. It is exhausting. And it is largely fake.

And then, there's the guilt. If you are reading this (or listening to this), you are probably the type of person who gives a damn. You recycle. You bring your tote bag to the grocery store. You worry about the ice caps.

You are familiar with the concept of *flygskam* - flight shame. You know that every time you step onto a plane, you are punching a hole in the atmosphere. It creates a nasty little knot of cognitive dissonance in your chest. You want to see the world before it burns, but you're terrified that by seeing it, you're holding the match.

So, what are your options?

Option A: You stop traveling. You stay home, tend your garden, and resign yourself to a life of vicarious living through documentaries. (Boring. Unrealistic. Depressing.)

Option B: You ignore the guilt. You book the flight, buy the plastic water bottle, stay at the chain resort, and tell yourself that one person doesn't make a difference. (Lazy. Destructive. Also depressing.)

I am proposing Option C.

The Solution: The Art of the Dupe

In the world of fashion or makeup, a "dupe" is a knock-off. It's the cheap imitation of the expensive original. You buy the dupe because you can't afford the real thing.

But in the world of travel, the definition is flipped.

In travel, the "Dupe" is the *original* experience. It is the place as it existed before the crowds ruined it. It is the authentic reality that the "Tourist Trap" is trying to sell you a plastic version of.

Venice is the trap; Treviso is the Dupe.

Bali is the trap; Lombok is the Dupe.

Tulum is the trap; Bacalar is the Dupe.

The Dupe is where the food actually tastes like the region. It's where the money you spend stays in the pocket of the family who cooked your dinner, rather than being wired to a corporate account in Switzerland. It is where you are not a consumer of a destination, but a participant in it.

This book is your field guide to finding those places. It is a manifesto for the "Dupe Hunter."

The Promise: Progress, Not Perfection

Let's get one thing clear before we go any further: This is not a lecture.

I am not going to yell at you for taking a plane. I am not going to suggest that the only "ethical" way to travel is to walk to Mongolia or sleep in a yurt—unless, of course, that's your kink.

We are tired of preachy sustainability books that treat travel like a sin. They demand perfection, and when perfection feels impossible, most people just give up.

This book is about the "Imperfect Advocate". It is about realizing that you don't have to be a saint to make a difference. You just have to be a little bit smarter.

We are going to focus on the "Wallet Wins," the "Planet Wins," and the "Vibe Checks." We are going to look at sustainability not as a sacrifice, but as a life hack. We are going to show you that the sustainable choice is almost always the cheaper choice, and weirdly enough, it is almost always the more luxurious choice.

Because here is the truth that the travel industry doesn't want you to know: Luxury isn't a thread count. Luxury is time. Luxury is space. Luxury is silence. Luxury is being the only person on the beach.

And you can't buy that luxury at a resort. You have to hunt for it.

How This Book Works

We are going to strip down your travel habits and rebuild them.

In **Chapter 1**, we're going to tackle the mindset. We'll look at why "Perfect" is the enemy of "Good" and why doing *something* is infinitely better than doing nothing.

In **Chapter 2**, we're going to get technical. I'm going to teach you how to hack Google Flights and reverse-engineer Instagram to find destinations that the algorithm is hiding from you.

In **Chapter 3**, we're going to learn how to spot a liar. We'll hand you a "Greenwashing Detection Kit" so you can tell the difference between a hotel that actually cares about the planet and one that just wants to save money on laundry by not washing your towels.

Then, we're going to dive into the Dupes. We will break down the "European Swap" and the "Tropical Swap," giving you specific, actionable alternatives to the world's most overcrowded hotspots. We'll run the numbers—the cost savings and the carbon savings—so you can see exactly what you're winning.

We're going to talk about "Rawdogging" flights (yes, really) and the rebellion of Silent Travel. We're going to make trains sexy again with the concept of *Tagskryt*—train bragging. And we're going to show you how to eat like a local without getting food poisoning or getting ripped off.

The Contract

But first, you have to make a deal. Not with me. With yourself.

Turn the page (or scroll down) to the "Carbon Ledger." This is your contract. It says that you are done with being a passive tourist. It says that you are ready to stop consuming the world and start experiencing it. It says that you are willing to embrace the weird, the slow, and the unfamiliar.

It says that you are ready to save money, save your sanity, and slash your footprint.

The world is still big. It is still beautiful. And there are still secrets out there, if you know where to look.

Grab your bag. Let's go hunting.

Chapter 1: The Hunter's Mindset: Why "Perfect" is the Enemy of "Good"

Let's talk about the voice in your head.

You know the one. It's the voice that pipes up the moment you open Skyscanner. It's the voice that sounds suspiciously like a judgmental teenager on TikTok or an overly aggressive climate scientist.

You type in "Tokyo," and the voice whispers: "Do you know how much jet fuel that burns? You monster."

You look at a boutique hotel, and the voice says: "I bet they don't even compost. You're part of the problem."

This is the Guilt Trap

It's a specific flavor of neurosis known as "Eco-Anxiety," and if you are reading this book, you probably have a severe case of it. You are trapped in a binary nightmare. In one corner, you have the desire to see the world, to eat street food in Penang, to smell the sulfur in Iceland. In the other corner, you have the crushing weight of knowing that the planet is on fire.

The result? Paralysis.

You start believing that unless you can travel with zero impact - unless you can swim across the Atlantic and sleep in a hammock made of your own woven hair - you shouldn't travel at all. You convince yourself that because you can't do it *perfectly*, you shouldn't do it.

Here is the cold, hard truth: **Sustainability is not a purity test. It is a practice.**

If we wait for perfection, we will never leave the house. And frankly, a world where the only people traveling are the ones who *don't* give a damn about the environment is a terrifying prospect. We need you out there. But we need you to change how you play the game.

The "Imperfect" Advocate

We need to make a deal right now. You are going to give yourself permission to fly.

Yes, planes emit carbon. Yes, tourism has flaws. But simply opting out of the world doesn't save it. It just leaves the world to the people who are happy to pave paradise to put up a parking lot.

The goal of the Dupe Hunter is not "Zero Choices." It is "Better Choices.". It is about being an **Imperfect Advocate**.

An imperfect advocate is someone who knows they are going to leave a footprint, so they decide to make sure that footprint is worth it. They decide to make it count. They realize that striving for 100% sustainability leads to mental breakdown, whereas striving for 70% sustainability actually leads to change.

Let me tell you a story about why "Perfect" is overrated, and why "Real" is what we are actually chasing.

The Tale of the Failed Eco-Trip

A few years ago, I went on a trip that, on paper, was a disaster.

It was a small eco-lodge in the rainforest, miles from the nearest paved road. It wasn't the "Eco-Lodge" you see on Instagram with the infinity pool and the acai bowls. It was the real kind. The kind where the electricity cut out at 8:00 PM and the shower was a pipe sticking out of a rock that dispensed water at precisely two temperatures: freezing and "why is this freezing?"

It rained for four days straight. Not a drizzle. A biblical deluge. The kind of rain that makes you wonder if you should start gathering animals two by two.

The roof of my hut leaked. There was a spider the size of a dinner plate that lived near the toilet, and we formed a respectful, non-verbal treaty regarding territory. I spent half the trip damp, muddy, and smelling like wet dog.

By standard tourism metrics, this was a failure. It was uncomfortable. It was inconvenient.

But down the coast, there was a massive all-inclusive resort. I knew what was happening there. The air conditioning was blasting at 68 degrees. The buffet was serving imported strawberries that had flown further than the guests. The tourists were drinking Piña Coladas in a sanitized, hermetically sealed bubble, completely oblivious to the country they were actually in.

In my leaky hut, I was miserable, sure. But I was also *present*.

Because I was stuck there, I ended up drinking coffee with the owner, a guy who used the lodge's meager profits to fight illegal logging in the valley. I learned how the rain affected the local river systems. I ate fish that his brother caught that morning.

That trip didn't look like a postcard. It felt like *life*.

The resort travelers bought a product. I had an experience. Their money went to a corporation; my money went to keeping a forest standing. It was messy, it was imperfect, and it was infinitely better than the sterile alternative.

That is the vibe we are chasing. We aren't trying to be comfortable. We are trying to be conscious.

The 3 Rules of the Hunt

So, how do we operationalize this? How do we move from "feeling guilty" to "doing good"?

You need a code. A set of rules to keep you from falling into the tourist traps that suck your wallet dry and choke the planet.

Rule 1: Go Where They Aren't

If you remember nothing else from this book, remember this: **Dispersal is the number one sustainable act**.

Overtourism is just a concentration problem. It's 10,000 people trying to stand on the same bridge in Venice at the same time. It destroys the infrastructure, infuriates the locals, and turns the destination into a theme park.

The Dupe Hunter looks at the crowd and walks the other way.

If everyone is going to Santorini, you go to Folegandros. If everyone is going to Tulum, you go to Bacalar. You aren't just doing this to be a hipster contrarian (though, let's be honest, it feels good). You are doing it to physically spread the load.

You are taking your economic power and moving it to a place that actually needs it, rather than a place that is drowning in it. You are trading a queue for a conversation. You are trading a selfie for a memory.

Rule 2: Stay Longer

Let's talk math. Specifically, the math of the "Slowmad".

We have been conditioned to treat travel like a smash-and-grab robbery. We fly in on Friday, hit the main sights on Saturday, hungover brunch on Sunday, fly out.

This is terrible for your soul, and it is catastrophic for your carbon footprint.

Taking four flights for four separate weekend trips is an environmental disaster. Taking *one* flight and staying for a month? That is a completely different equation.

The takeoff and landing are the most carbon-intensive parts of the journey. When you stay longer, you dilute the impact of that flight over more days. You sink into the rhythm of a place. You stop rushing. You start living.

The goal is depth, not breadth. Stop counting countries. Start counting mornings waking up in the same bed, learning the name of the guy who sells you bread.

Rule 3: Spend Local

There is an economic term called "Leakage." It sounds like a plumbing problem, and it basically is.

In traditional mass tourism, for every $100 you spend in a developing country, only about $5 to $10 stays in that country. The rest - the other $90 - leaks out. It goes to foreign-owned hotel chains, international tour operators, and imported food logistics.

This is why you see luxury resorts surrounded by poverty. The money is literally flying away.

The Dupe Hunter focuses on Injection.

When you eat at a local *taverna*, sleep in a locally owned guesthouse, and hire a local guide, that money stays. It circulates. It builds schools, it fixes roads, it puts food on tables.

This is the most powerful tool you have. Your credit card is a weapon. You can use it to support a corporate extraction machine, or you can use it to water the roots of a community.

Workbook Element: The "Traveler vs. Tourist" Self-Audit

Alright, time to look in the mirror.

This isn't a Cosmo quiz to find out which "Sex and the City" character you are. This is a reality check. Grab a pen, or just make a mental note. Be honest. Nobody is watching.

1. **When you book accommodation, do you check who owns it?**
    - *Tourist:* No, I just look for the cheapest price and the highest thread count.

    - *Traveler:* Yes, I look for "family-run" or locally owned indicators.

2. How fast do you move?

- *Tourist:* If it's Tuesday, this must be Belgium. I need to hit 3 cities in 5 days.
- *Traveler:* I have no idea what day it is, but I know the fishmonger's schedule.

3. What do you eat?

- *Tourist:* I look for places with pictures on the menu or a familiar burger joint.
- *Traveler:* I eat what the locals are eating, even if I have to Google translate the menu and it turns out to be "spicy tripe."

4. How do you handle "The Ick"?

- *Tourist:* If the WiFi is slow or there's a bug, I leave a 1-star review.
- *Traveler:* I realize that I am a guest in someone else's home, and sometimes, homes have bugs.

If you answered mostly "Tourist," don't panic. That's why you bought this book. We are going to deprogram that behavior. We are going to turn you into a hunter.

The perfectionism stops here. The guilt stops here. The adventure begins now.

Chapter 2: The Search Engine Strategy: Hacking the System

Here is a hard truth that the travel industry spends billions of dollars trying to hide from you: **The algorithm hates you.**

Okay, maybe it doesn't *hate* you personally. It doesn't know you exist. But it is indifferent to your happiness, your wallet, and the planet. The travel algorithm—the complex web of cookies, SEO, and paid placements that dictates what you see when you type "vacation" into a search bar—has one job. Its job is to funnel you into the same high-margin, high-traffic chutes as everyone else.

It wants you in the $400-a-night Marriott in Maui. It wants you on the overcrowded flight to Heathrow. It wants you to be a predictable, efficient unit of consumption.

Most people play right into this. They sit down, open their laptops, and type: *"Flights to Paris, July 1st to July 7th."*

Do you see the problem? You just handed all your leverage to the airline. You told them exactly *where* you want to go and exactly *when* you want to be there. You are a captive audience. Of course the price is going to be astronomical. Of course the flight is going to be full. You are fishing in a barrel, but you're the fish.

If you want to be a Dupe Hunter, you have to stop searching like a tourist and start searching like a hacker. You have to break the pattern.

We are going to reverse the entire process. Instead of asking, *"How much does it cost to go where everyone else is going?"* we are going to ask, *"Where can I live like a king for the $500 I actually have?"*

The Tool: The "Map View" Supremacy

The greatest tool in the sustainable traveler's arsenal is not a reusable straw. It is the **Google Flights "Explore" map view**.

Most people use Google Flights like a bus schedule. They punch in A and B.

I want you to leave "B" blank.

Here is the strategy:

1. Open Google Flights.

2. Enter your home airport.

3. Leave the destination **blank** (or select "Anywhere").

4. Click "Search."

Suddenly, you aren't looking at a list of prices for a single city. You are looking at a map of the world, covered in price tags.

This is the "God View."

You might see that flying to Rome costs $1,200. But look two inches to the left. Flying to **Nice** is $450. Look a bit to the right. **Tirana, Albania** is $380.

Now we are cooking.

This requires a fundamental shift in mindset. You have to detach your ego from a specific destination. If you are dead-set on "Santorini or Bust," you are going to go bust. But if you are open to "The Mediterranean Vibe," the map will show you the backdoors.

Maybe you find a flight to **Bologna** instead of Florence. Bologna is the culinary heart of Italy. It's where the locals actually eat. The streets are medieval terracotta red, the ragù is a religious experience, and you aren't fighting a tour group for sidewalk space. And you just saved $600 on airfare.

That $600 isn't just "savings." That is your budget for the entire week of eating. That is the difference between a stress-filled vacation and a glorious one.

By searching by **price**, not destination, you are essentially short-circuiting the industry's pricing algorithms[4]. You are picking off the empty seats they are desperate to fill, rather than fighting for the seats everyone wants.

The Algorithm: Visual Hacking

Let's talk about Instagram.

We all claim we don't care about "doing it for the 'Gram," but we're lying. We are visual creatures. We see a photo of a wooden dock stretching out into turquoise water, and our lizard brain says: *"I want to go to there."*

The problem is, everyone sees the *same* photo. That dock is probably in the Maldives, and staying there costs a kidney.

But here is the hack: **Reverse-Image Search**.

Take that photo of the expensive, crowded paradise you lust after. Screenshot it. Then, upload it to Google Images or Pinterest's visual search tool.

The algorithm will spit back visually similar images. But here is the magic: it won't just show you the Maldives. It will show you everywhere *else* in the world that looks like that.

You might see a photo that looks identical—same turquoise water, same white sand—but the caption says **"Bacalar, Mexico"** or **"Koh Rong, Cambodia."**

Suddenly, you have a lead.

You have found a "Dupe" based purely on aesthetics. The water is just as blue. The sand is just as white. But the price tag is missing a zero, and the carbon footprint to get there might be half.

This is how you find the places that haven't blown up yet. You are using the visual data against itself. You are finding the "Hardware" (the landscape) without the "Software" (the expensive brand name).

Section: Timing the Market

If "Where" is the first variable we hack, "When" is the second.

The travel industry relies on the fact that human beings are creatures of habit. We all want to go to Europe in July. We all want to go to the Caribbean in

December. This is called "Peak Season," but a more accurate name would be "Rip-Off Season."

The Dupe Hunter lives in the **Shoulder Season**.

Shoulder season is that magical window between the peak and the off-peak. For Europe, it's May/June and September/October. The weather is still perfect—you can still wear a t-shirt, you can still drink wine outside—but the crowds have vanished.

In July, Venice is a mosh pit. In October, Venice is a melancholic, misty, heartbreakingly beautiful dream. And the hotels are 40% cheaper.

But there is a new trend you need to know about, driven by the reality of our warming planet: **"Coolcations"**.

It used to be that everyone chased the heat. But have you been to Southern Europe in August lately? It is 40°C (104°F). It is miserable. You aren't "sunning yourself"; you are being sous-vide cooked in your own sweat. The Acropolis closes at noon because people are literally fainting.

The new "flex" isn't heat. It's **temperate comfort**.

Smart travelers are heading North. They are going to Scandinavia, Scotland, the Baltics, or high-altitude mountain regions in the summer. They are chasing 70°F (21°C) days where you can actually hike, walk, and breathe.

Searching for "Coolcations" allows you to zag while the rest of the world zigs. While your friends are complaining about the heat wave in Seville, you are wearing a light sweater on a ferry in the Norwegian fjords, breathing the cleanest air on earth.

That isn't just sustainable; it's superior.

Action Steps: Setting the Trap

You now understand the philosophy. Here is the tactical checklist to execute the hunt.

1. The "Everywhere" Alert

Go to **Skyscanner**. Set up an alert. But don't set it for a specific route. Use the **"Explore Everywhere"** function.

You want to know when *any* price drops. You want to be notified that, suddenly, flights to Guatemala are $200.

This turns travel planning from a "Search" (active effort) into a "Notification" (passive opportunity). You let the deals come to you. You wait for the system to glitch in your favor.

2. The "3-Click Rule" for Logistics

Once you find a potential Dupe—say, a small beach town in Albania—you need to vet it. Is it accessible, or is it a logistical nightmare that will require a private helicopter?

Use the **3-Click Rule** for local transport info.

Try to find a bus or train schedule from the airport to the town.

- **Click 1:** Google Maps directions.
- **Click 2:** The official local transport website (e.g., Rome2Rio or the local bus line).
- **Click 3:** A recent blog or forum post confirming it actually runs.

If you can't find a reliable way to get there in three clicks (or three layers of digging), pause.

Now, a "Tourist" would give up here. A "Dupe Hunter" might get excited.

Hard-to-find info is often the natural barrier that keeps the crowds away. If you can't find the bus schedule online, it means 10,000 other people couldn't find it either. That bus might be the best ride of your life.

However, if you are traveling with kids or have limited mobility, the 3-Click Rule is your safety valve. If the info isn't there, the infrastructure might not be there either. Know your limits.

Conclusion: The Blank Slate

The ultimate goal of this strategy is to reclaim your agency.

When you start typing "Anywhere" into the search bar, you stop being a consumer who is being sold a vacation package. You become an explorer who is choosing an adventure.

You stop measuring your trip against what your friends did or what the algorithm told you to want. You start measuring it by the value you get, the connections you make, and the money you save.

The system is designed to make you predictable.

Be unpredictable.

The map is wide open.

Now, let's look at how to make sure that "Eco-Lodge" you found isn't just a greenwashed lie. Turn the page.

Chapter 3: The "Eco-Lodge" or The "Eco-Lie"? Detecting Greenwashing

You've seen the place. It's on Instagram right now.

It calls itself "The Gaia Sanctuary" or "Pure Earth Retreat." The website features photos of a woman in white linen laughing at a salad. There is a lot of bamboo. The font is thin and sans-serif. The copy uses words like "holistic," "unplugged," and "symbiotic."

It costs $800 a night.

But when you actually get there, something feels... off.

You notice the "locally sourced" fruit is perfectly uniform and has stickers from a multinational conglomerate. You notice the air conditioning is blasting so hard you could store sides of beef in the lobby. You notice that the "lush tropical gardens" are actually non-native thirsty plants being kept alive by a sprinkler system running at high noon in a region suffering from a drought.

And then you see it. The single-use plastic water bottle. But wait! It's wrapped in brown butcher paper with a little twine bow.

Congratulations. You have been greenwashed.

This isn't an eco-lodge. It's a hotel in a costume. It is a cynical cash grab designed to separate well-meaning people from their money by exploiting their desire not to destroy the planet.

This is the "Eco-Lie." And in this chapter, we are going to learn how to sniff it out, dismantle it, and avoid funding it.

The Great Towel Scam

Let's start with the oldest trick in the book. You know the little placard in the bathroom. It usually has a picture of a turtle or a leaf on it. It says something like:

"Dear Guest, Mother Earth is tired. Please hang up your towel if you want to save the planet. Leave it on the floor if you hate dolphins."

Let's be real for a second.

"We don't wash towels" is cost-cutting, not conservation.

Sure, saving water is good. I'm not saying you should use a fresh towel every time you wash your face. But when a massive hotel chain makes this their *only* sustainability initiative, they aren't doing it for the turtles. They are doing it for the bottom line. They are saving tens of thousands of dollars a year on labor, water, electricity, and detergent.

If a hotel asks you to reuse your towel but still serves dinner on disposable plates, has no solar panels, and waters a golf course in the desert, that placard is just a prop. It's gaslighting. It's shifting the burden of sustainability onto *you*, the paying guest, while the corporation changes absolutely nothing about its infrastructure.

Don't applaud them for it. It's the bare minimum. It's like a chef bragging that he didn't poison your soup.

The "Ick": Performative Sustainability

Greenwashing has become sophisticated. It used to be easy to spot, but now marketing teams are getting better at faking the "vibe" of sustainability without doing the work.

This creates a specific feeling I call "The Ick."

The Ick is that creeping suspicion that you are being played. It's identifying performative sustainability - like the brown paper wrapped around plastic.

I once stayed at a "jungle eco-retreat" that bragged about being "plastic-free." And they were, technically. In the room. But I walked around the back of the kitchen and saw a mountain of Styrofoam containers and plastic wrap. They weren't reducing waste; they were just hiding it from the guests. They were curating an aesthetic, not an ecosystem.

True sustainability isn't aesthetic. It's often ugly. It's compost bins that smell a little earthy. It's showers that have low pressure. It's furniture that doesn't match because it was repaired rather than replaced.

If a place looks too perfect, too polished, and too manicured, your radar should be pinging. Nature is messy. If the "Eco-Lodge" feels like a sterile operating room with some bamboo glued to the walls, run.

The Greenwashing Detection Kit

So, how do you find the real deal?

You have to stop being a passive consumer and start being an investigator. You need to look under the hood. You need a **Greenwashing Detection Kit**.

This doesn't mean you have to be aggressive. You don't need to storm the front desk and demand to see the utility bills. But you do need to ask the right questions before you book.

Here is "The Interrogation" - three questions that cut through the marketing fluff.

Question 1: "Where does your greywater go?"

This is the killer question.

Most hotel managers will blink at you. They won't know. Or they'll mumble something about the municipal sewer.

But a *real* eco-lodge? Their eyes will light up. They will tell you about their reed bed filtration system. They will explain how the water from the showers is filtered through volcanic rock and used to water the banana trees. They will offer to show you the pipes.

Greywater management is unsexy. It's expensive. It's invisible. No marketing team puts a picture of a septic tank on the homepage. That's why it's the perfect litmus test. If they are doing this, they are doing it for the right reasons.

Question 2: "What percentage of your management team is local?"

Notice I said *management*.

A lot of hotels hire locals to clean the toilets and trim the hedges, while the General Manager, the Chef, and the Concierge are flown in from Europe or the US.

That's not sustainable tourism; that's colonialism with a concierge desk.

You want to hear that the decision-makers are local. You want to hear that there is a path for advancement. If the hotel is owned by a foreign investment firm and run by expats, the money is leaking out of the community faster than you can say "all-inclusive."

Question 3: "How do you support the local community beyond employment?"

The fake answer: "We give our leftover food to a pig farm."

The real answer: "We source 80% of our ingredients from farmers within 20 miles," or "We built the local primary school," or "We sponsor a turtle hatchery."

You are looking for **integration**, not just occupation.

The Certification Jungle

"But wait," you ask. "Can't I just trust the little logos at the bottom of the website?"

Welcome to the **Certification Jungle**.

There are over 200 "sustainable travel" labels out there. Most of them are garbage. They are "pay-to-play" schemes where a hotel sends a check and gets a shiny "Green Leaf Award" PDF to put on their footer. They are marketing, not auditing.

However, there are a few sheriffs in town that actually carry a gun. You need to learn to recognize the logos that actually matter.

- **B Corp:** This is the gold standard. It means the entire business structure is legally required to prioritize social and environmental impact, not just profit. It is incredibly hard to get. If you see a B Corp logo, you can relax.

- **GSTC (Global Sustainable Tourism Council):** These guys set the global baseline standards. They don't certify hotels directly, but they accredit the certifiers. Look for "GSTC-Recognized" standards.

- **EarthCheck / Green Key:** These are legitimate, third-party audits. They actually send a guy with a clipboard to check the water meters.

If the certification is something generic like "World Luxury Green Awards," be skeptical. Google it. If the application process involves a credit card form and no site visit, it's a scam.

Red Flags vs. Green Flags

We're going to make this easy for you. When you are scrolling through Booking.com or looking at a hotel's website, use this checklist. This is your "Greenwashing Detection Kit" cheat sheet[7].

The Red Flags (The "Run Away" List)

- **The "Desert Oasis":** Exotic, water-guzzling plants (like English roses or lush lawns) in an arid environment.

- **The Single-Use Swap:** Replacing plastic bottles with glass bottles... that are still single-use and imported from Italy.

- **The "Eco-Activities":** Offering jet ski tours, ATV rides through the jungle, or "swimming with dolphins" in a tank.
- **The Mystery Menu:** A restaurant that serves salmon in the tropics or beef in a region where cows don't live.
- **The Air-Con Freeze:** Lobbies and open spaces that are air-conditioned to arctic temperatures with the doors wide open.

The Green Flags (The "Book It" List)

- **Native Landscaping:** The gardens look like the surrounding nature (succulents in the desert, wild grasses in the plains). They don't need excessive water.
- **Refill Stations:** Not just "no plastic," but actual water cooler stations where you can fill your own bottle.
- **Passive Cooling:** Architecture designed to catch the breeze (high ceilings, cross-ventilation) so you don't *need* the AC constantly.
- **Seasonal Menus:** A menu that changes based on what is growing nearby. "No avocados today because they aren't ripe" is a massive green flag.
- **Community Presence:** You see the hotel promoting *other* local businesses recommending a nearby restaurant rather than trying to keep you trapped in the resort.

Conclusion: Vote With Your Wallet

Here is the bottom line.

Every time you book a hotel, you are casting a vote for the kind of world you want to see.

If you book the fake eco-resort because it looks pretty on TikTok, you are telling the industry: *"Please lie to me. I don't care about the reality, I just want the aesthetic."*

But when you ask the hard questions - when you email them about greywater, when you check for the B Corp logo, when you choose the locally owned guest-house over the foreign chain - you are sending a different message. You are saying: *"I see you. I value the work you are doing. And I am willing to pay for it."*

The "Eco-Lie" only works if we are lazy. Don't be lazy. Be a hunter.

Now that you know where to stay, let's talk about where to go. It's time to look at the map and swap the "Tourist Traps" for the "Dupes." Turn the page to the **European Swap**.

The "Greenwashing" Betrayal

I want to tell you about the exact moment I lost my innocence. It wasn't in a dark alley or a shady deal gone wrong. It was in a patch of jungle that smelled like sandalwood, money, and lies.

It happened three years ago. I was deep in the throes of what I call "The Pinterest Delusion." I was burnt out, over-caffeinated, and desperate for an escape that felt virtuous. I didn't just want a vacation; I wanted a spiritual reset. I wanted to go somewhere where the architecture would heal me and the breakfast bowl would align my chakras.

I found it on Instagram, of course. It was a place in Tulum we'll call "The Gaia Sanctuary." The photos were lethal. There were thatched roofs made of sustainable palm fronds. There were women in white linen dresses floating through candlelit walkways. The copy on the website was written in a font so thin it looked like it was whispering secrets about carbon neutrality. It used words like *symbiotic*, *off-grid*, and *ancestral wisdom*. It cost six hundred dollars a night.

I booked it immediately. I remember feeling a distinct wave of smugness as I entered my credit card information. I told myself I wasn't just buying a hotel room; I was investing in the planet. I was paying the "Eco-Premium" to ensure that my presence wouldn't hurt the local ecosystem. I was a good person. I was a *conscious* traveler.

I was an idiot.

The cracks started showing the moment I checked in. The lobby was stunning, I'll give them that. It was an open-air cathedral of bamboo and polished concrete, smelling intensely of burning copal incense. But beneath the incense, there was something else. A faint, acrid undercurrent. It smelled like a mechanic's garage on a hot day. I ignored it. I accepted my welcome drink - a green juice served in a heavy, hand-blown glass - and let the receptionist with the perfect messy bun lead me to my "Jungle Casita."

The room was beautiful, in that sparse, expensive way that suggests furniture is a burden to the soul. But it was hot. Oppressively, violently hot. When I asked about the air conditioning, the receptionist smiled at me with the pity one reserves for a toddler who asks for candy before dinner.

"We are an eco-sanctuary," she purred. "We rely on the natural rhythms of the wind. The architecture is designed for passive cooling."

Passive cooling is a lovely concept in a textbook. In a concrete box in the Mexican jungle at 90% humidity, passive cooling is just a fancy term for being sous-vide cooked in your own sweat. But I nodded. I didn't want to be the high-maintenance American. I wanted to be the breezy, eco-conscious nomad. So I unpacked my bag, lay down on the damp sheets, and tried to meditate.

That's when I heard it.

It was a low, rhythmic thrumming. *Thump-thump-thump-thump.* It vibrated through the floorboards. It rattled the artisanal ceramic water jug on the nightstand. It wasn't the ocean. It wasn't the wind. It sounded like a massive, angry heart buried somewhere beneath the sand.

By midnight, I couldn't take it anymore. The heat was suffocating, and the thumping had burrowed into my skull. I needed water, and I needed to know what the hell that noise was. I grabbed my flashlight and stepped out onto the path.

The resort was deserted. The candles had burned low. I followed the sound. I walked past the yoga shala, past the vegan restaurant, and past the "Sacred Cenote" swimming hole. The path turned from crushed white shell to dirt. The landscaping got messy. The bamboo walls got higher, clearly meant to block the view.

I slipped through a gap in the fence, and there it was. The heart of darkness.

It wasn't a wind turbine. It wasn't a solar array. It was a diesel generator the size of a school bus. It was roaring, shaking the ground, spewing a thick, black plume of exhaust directly into the canopy of the jungle.

I stood there, freezing in the tropical heat, staring at this industrial monster. Beside it were stacked jerry cans of fuel, leaking rainbow puddles into the soil. This was the "off-grid" power source. This was the "ancestral wisdom." The entire resort - the lights, the blenders making the $18 smoothies, the pumps for the infinity pool - was running on dirty diesel fuel, burned 24 hours a day to maintain the illusion of rustic simplicity.

But that wasn't the worst part.

Movement caught my eye near the service entrance. A young staff member was working under a floodlight. He was surrounded by crates. I watched, mesmerized by the horror, as he picked up a generic, single-use plastic gallon jug of water - the kind you buy at Costco for a dollar. He unscrewed the cap and poured it into one of the resort's signature "Eco-Glass" carafes. He did it again. And again. When the plastic jug was empty, he crushed it and threw it onto a pile of hundreds of other crushed plastic jugs.

I felt a physical kick to the stomach. The "locally filtered, zero-waste" water they left in my room? It was just plastic-bottled water, rebranded. They weren't saving the planet from plastic; they were just hiding the plastic from *me*. They were performing sustainability as aesthetic theater.

I walked back to my room in a daze. The smell of the copal incense suddenly made me nauseous. I realized it wasn't there to set a mood; it was there to mask the smell of the diesel exhaust.

I lay in bed that night, listening to the generator roar, and I felt a profound sense of betrayal. It wasn't just about the money, though $600 a night is a steep price to pay to be lied to. It was the cynicism of it. They knew exactly what I wanted. They knew I carried the guilt of my privilege like a heavy backpack. They knew I was desperate to believe that I could enjoy luxury without consequences.

And they had weaponized that desire against me.

They had built a stage set. The bamboo, the linen, the "passive cooling" - it was all a costume. The "Eco-Lodge" was essentially a factory in the woods, running on fossil fuels and single-use plastic, but charging double the price of the Marriott down the road because they had wrapped the deception in brown butcher paper and tied it with a piece of twine.

I checked out the next morning. When the receptionist asked how my stay was, asking if I felt "reconnected," I looked her dead in the eye. I wanted to scream. I wanted to drag her out back to the generator and point at the black smoke choking the palm trees.

But I didn't. I just paid the bill. I realized then that the anger I was feeling wasn't just at them. It was at myself. I had been lazy. I had fallen for the vibe instead of checking the facts. I had treated sustainability as a purchase I could make, rather than a practice I had to verify.

That was the moment the "Dupe Hunter" was born. As I walked out of the Gaia Sanctuary, dragging my suitcase through the dust, I promised myself I would never be a mark again. I realized that if you want to find the truth in travel, you have to stop looking at the brochure and start looking at the plumbing. You have to ignore the font and look for the generator.

I walked down the road to a small, locally owned guesthouse I found on Google Maps. It wasn't on Instagram. The sheets didn't match. But there was a solar heater on the roof, the owner was working the front desk, and the breeze coming through the window was real. It cost $50 a night.

I slept like a baby.

Chapter 4: The European Swap: Champagne Vibes on a Beer Budget

Let's be honest about the "European Summer."

Somewhere along the line, a marketing executive sold us a lie. They sold us a vision of Europe that consists of riding a Vespa through an empty cobblestone street, sipping an Aperol Spritz with a supermodel, and watching the sunset in profound, spiritual silence. They sold us *La Dolce Vita*.

But if you go to Europe in July without a plan, you aren't getting *La Dolce Vita*. You are getting *La Dolce Sweat-a*.

You are getting body-checked by a tour group from Ohio on the Rialto Bridge. You are paying €12 for a Coca-Cola that is mostly ice. You are standing in a queue for the Louvre that is longer than the actual reign of Louis XIV. You are hemorrhaging money, sweating through your linen shirt, and wondering why the "Old World" smells so much like sunscreen and despair.

This is the "Tourist Trap" reality.

The great tragedy of modern travel is that we all want the same thing at the same time. We all read the same "Top 10" lists. We all follow the same influencers. And in doing so, we destroy the very thing we came to find. We turn living cities into open-air museums, and we turn ourselves into walking wallets.

But here is the good news: The Europe you are dreaming of still exists.

The quiet piazzas, the cheap wine that tastes like god, the mountains that haven't been geotagged into oblivion—they are all still there. They are just slightly to the left.

We call this The European Swap.

This is the art of the "Dupe." It's about getting the Champagne vibe—the luxury, the beauty, the history—on a Beer budget. And more importantly, on a Beer carbon footprint.

We are going to look at three of the biggest "Traps" in Europe—Venice, the Swiss Alps, and Santorini—and we are going to swap them for destinations that offer the same hardware (scenery, architecture, food) without the buggy software (crowds, prices, guilt).

We are going to stop being tourists, and start being guests.

Part I: The Canal Conundrum

The Trap: Venice

(The Sinking Disneyland)

Venice is a miracle. Let's not pretend it isn't. It is a city built on wood piles driven into a marsh, a marble hallucination floating on water. It is one of the most significant achievements of human engineering and art.

It is also, currently, a nightmare.

If you go to Venice in the summer, you are not visiting a city. You are visiting a theme park where the employees are grumpy Italians who wish you would leave. The "Bridge of Sighs" is appropriately named, because that is what you will be doing while you are wedged between a backpacker and a stone wall for forty-five minutes.

Venice is sinking, both geologically and metaphorically. It is sinking under the weight of day-trippers. The canals, which should be romantic arteries of the city, are traffic jams of gondolas, water taxis, and garbage barges. In the heat of

August, the water doesn't smell like the Adriatic; it smells like a wet dog wrapped in seaweed and left in a sauna.

And the cost? You will pay a "tourist tax" on everything. A coffee in St. Mark's Square costs as much as a used car. The food, by and large, is cynical. It's "Menu Turistico" garbage—frozen lasagna and rubbery calamari served to people who they know will never come back.

Venice is a place you go to say you've been, not a place you go to *be.*

The Dupe: Treviso

(The Prosecco Road)

Twenty minutes away by train—a train that costs less than a cappuccino—lies Treviso.

If Venice is the fading, makeup-caked movie star trying to relive her glory days, Treviso is her cooler, younger sister who works in fashion and knows where the good parties are.

Treviso has canals. Beautiful ones. They wind through the city, flanked by weeping willows and water wheels. The architecture is Venetian Gothic, with frescoed facades that haven't been scrubbed clean for a postcard.

But here is the difference: **People actually live here.**

When you sit down at a cafe in the Piazza dei Signori, the people at the next table aren't from Des Moines. They are from Treviso. They are arguing about soccer. They are reading the paper. They are drinking *Ombra* (small glasses of wine) at 11:00 AM because that is the civilized thing to do.

Treviso is the gateway to the "Prosecco Road," the rolling hills where Italy's most famous bubbles are born. Here, the Prosecco isn't a markup; it's a birthright. You can walk into a tavern and get a glass of Glera (the sparkling wine of the region) for €2 or €3. It's crisp, it's cold, and it tastes like victory.

The Culinary Flex:

Here is a fact you can drop to look smart: Treviso is the birthplace of Tiramisu.

In Venice, you get a thawing square of industrial cake. In Treviso, at a place like Le Beccherie, you get the original. It is a slap in the face of flavor—bitter espresso, sweet mascarpone, the crunch of the ladyfingers. It is messy and perfect.

The Wallet Win:

You are paying 50% less for accommodation that is 100% better. You aren't staying in a closet-sized room that smells like damp plaster. You are staying in a boutique hotel or an apartment where the host leaves you fresh bread.

The Planet Win:

Venice is fragile. Every footstep erodes the stone. Every boat wake erodes the foundations. By staying in Treviso and just visiting Venice for a day (or skipping it entirely), you are reducing the pressure on a dying city. You are dispersing the crowd.

The Alternative Dupe: Aveiro, Portugal

If your heart isn't set on Italy, but you crave the water-city aesthetic, look at **Aveiro, Portugal**.

They call it the "Venice of Portugal," which is lazy marketing, because Aveiro has its own thing going on. It has canals, yes. It has *Moliceiros* (colorful boats that look like gondolas on acid). But it also has Art Nouveau architecture that would make Gaudi jealous, and it is right next to the Atlantic Ocean.

It is salty, windy, and unpretentious. You eat *Ovos Moles* (sweet egg pastries), you drink Vinho Verde, and you don't feel like a intruder. You feel like you found a secret.

Part II: The Mountain Meltdown

The Trap: The Swiss Alps

(The Gold-Plated Postcard)

Switzerland is beautiful. It is aggressively, violently beautiful. The mountains look like they were chiseled by a perfectionist god. The grass is so green it looks radioactive. The trains run on time to the nanosecond.

But Switzerland has a problem: It is functionally bankrupting.

Unless you are a hedge fund manager or a minor royal, Switzerland is a financial panic attack waiting to happen. You sit down for a fondue—literally a pot of melted cheese and stale bread—and the bill comes to $40 per person. A train ticket up the mountain costs as much as a flight to Asia.

There is also a strange sterility to it. It is so perfect, so manicured, so orderly, that it sometimes feels like a simulation. It is nature under glass. You are hiking on trails that feel like they've been vacuumed. It's "glamping" on a national scale.

For the rugged traveler—for the "Conservation David" who wants stewardship and history, or the "Conscious Maya" who wants to feel wild—Switzerland can feel a bit... plastic wrapped.

The Dupe: The Accursed Mountains, Albania

(The Last Wilderness)

Let's talk about a place with a name so metal it belongs on an album cover: **The Accursed Mountains** (*Bjeshkët e Nemuna*).

Located in Northern Albania, bordering Montenegro and Kosovo, these mountains are what the Alps used to be fifty years ago. They are jagged, limestone teeth biting into the sky. They are wild, untamed, and spectacularly dramatic.

And they are a fraction of the cost.

Albania is the "Dupe" of the decade. After being closed off to the world under a paranoid communist dictatorship for forty years, it has swung its doors open, and it is hungry for visitors. But the mass tourism machine hasn't paved it over yet.

The Experience:

You don't stay in a chain hotel. You stay in a Guest House in the village of Theth or Valbona. These are old stone towers (Kullas) converted into homestays.

This is where you encounter the concept of *Besa*.

Besa is an ancient Albanian code of honor. It translates roughly to "promise" or "word of honor," but it means much more. It means that a guest is sacred. When you stay in Theth, the family doesn't just check you in; they feed you.

They feed you mountains of food. Lamb roasted over a fire. *Flija* (layers of crepe-like batter baked with cream). Tomatoes that taste like sunshine. Homemade raki (brandy) that could strip paint off a car but makes you love everyone at the table.

The Cost/Carbon Breakdown:

- **Switzerland:**
    - Cost: $350/day (minimum).
    - Vibe: Polished, expensive, crowded with tour buses at the base.
- **Albania:**
    - Cost: $50/day.
    - Vibe: Raw, hospitable, empty trails.

You are hiking through passes where you won't see another soul for hours. You are drinking water straight from the streams because it's that clean. You are supporting a family directly, putting cash into a rural economy that is rebuilding itself.

This is not "settling" for a lesser mountain range. This is upgrading to a better adventure. The Alps are for tourists. The Accursed Mountains are for travelers.

Part III: The Island Illusion

The Trap: Santorini

(The Sunset Circus)

Santorini is the face that launched a thousand influencer careers. The white caldera, the blue domes, the pink bougainvillea. It is the single most recognizable image of Greece.

And because of that, it is hell on earth.

I want you to picture the famous sunset in Oia. In your mind, it's romantic. In reality, it is a mosh pit. People start lining up three hours in advance to secure a spot on the castle walls. They are aggressive. They are sweaty. When the sun finally dips below the horizon, people *clap*. They applaud the sun for doing the thing it has done every day for 4.5 billion years. It is the cringiest moment in travel.

And then there are the cruise ships. They dump up to 10,000 people a day onto an island that has the infrastructure for 500. The narrow streets become impassable. The donkeys, forced to haul overweight tourists up the stairs in the baking heat, are miserable (and you should never, ever ride them).

Santorini is a stage set. It is beautiful to look at, but it is hollow to touch. You are paying a 500% markup for the privilege of being elbowed by a stranger.

The Dupe: Folegandros or Paros

(The True Cyclades)

If you want the white buildings, the blue sea, and the stark, wind-swept beauty of the Cyclades without the madness, you have two incredible options.

Option A: Folegandros (The "Silent" Dupe)

Folegandros doesn't have an airport. This is its best feature. It acts as a filter. The only way to get there is by ferry, which keeps the mass market crowds away.

Folegandros is a rock in the middle of the sea. It is dramatic, barren, and breathtaking. The main town, the *Chora*, is built into the walls of a medieval castle (*Kastro*). It is pedestrian-only.

Here, there are no cruise ships. There are just squares (*plateias*) shaded by plane trees, where you can sit for four hours with a book and a coffee, and nobody will ask you to move. The silence is heavy and sweet.

You walk up the zigzag path to the Church of Panagia at sunset. There are other people there, sure. But they aren't screaming. They aren't fighting for angles. They are just watching. It is communal, not competitive.

Option B: Paros (The "Cool" Dupe)

If Folegandros is a bit too sleepy for you, go to Paros.

Paros is what Mykonos was twenty years ago before it became a caricature of itself. Paros has the nightlife, the beach clubs, and the shopping, but it retains its soul.

Go to the fishing village of **Naoussa**. Yes, it's popular, but it's popular with Greeks. You sit right on the water's edge. The waves literally lap at your chair. You eat *Guna* (sun-dried mackerel) and grilled squid.

The "Vibe Check":

In Santorini, you feel like a wallet on legs. The locals are exhausted by you.

In Folegandros or Paros, you feel like a human being. The hospitality (filoxenia) is real. The waiter actually wants to know where you're from, not just how quickly he can turn the table.

Part IV: The Logistics: Tagskryt (Train Bragging)

Making the Journey the Flex

So, we have our Dupes. Treviso, Albania, Folegandros. But how do we get there without destroying the planet?

We are going to lean into a Swedish term: **Tagskryt**. It translates to "Train Bragging".

For the last twenty years, the "flex" was flying private or flying first class. But in the era of climate crisis, that's not a flex anymore. That's just embarrassing.

The new status symbol is the slow route. It's the photo of your legs stretched out in a train cabin, a book in your lap, the Alps blurring by the window. It says: *"I have time. I have taste. And I'm not roasting the planet to get where I'm going."*

The Route Strategy:

You can connect these Dupes using the European rail network, which is arguably the best piece of infrastructure humanity has ever built.

1. The Night Train Renaissance:

Instead of paying for a hotel and a flight, combine them. Take the Nightjet. You can sleep your way from Amsterdam to Zurich, or Vienna to Venice.

- *The Hack:* You save the cost of a hotel night. You arrive in the city center at 8:00 AM, refreshed (mostly), and ready to go. No airport security lines. No "liquids under 100ml" nonsense.

Getting to Albania without flying is an adventure, but it's a good one. You take the ferry from Bari (Italy) to Durrës (Albania).

- Imagine this: You spend the evening in Bari, eating Orecchiette pasta. You board the ferry. You sleep in a cabin. You wake up seeing the sun rise over the Albanian mountains. It is romantic in the way travel used to be romantic. It feels like a movie.

In Greece, the ferry is the bus. But it's a bus with a sun deck and beer. Taking the ferry from Athens (Piraeus) to Folegandros takes a few hours, but it forces you to slow down. You watch the islands drift by. You decompress. By the time you arrive, you have shed the city stress.

The "Man in Seat 61":

If you are intimidated by train schedules, there is one resource you need: The Man in Seat 61 (seat61.com). This guy is the patron saint of rail travel. He explains every route, every ticket machine, every connection. Use it. It's the bible of Tagskryt.

Part V: The Breakdown

Cost & Carbon: The Cold Hard Data

We promised you Champagne vibes on a Beer budget. Let's look at the receipts.

We aren't just making this up. When you look at the **Cost/Carbon Breakdown**, the numbers are staggering.

The Venetian Swap:

- **Venice (The Trap):**
  - Avg Hotel: $350/night.
  - Avg Dinner: $60/person.
  - Carbon (Short Haul Flight): ~150kg CO2.
- **Treviso (The Dupe):**
  - Avg Hotel: $120/night. (**Savings: $230/night**)
  - Avg Dinner: $25/person. (**Savings: $35/meal**)
  - Carbon (Train): ~15kg CO2. (**Savings: 90%**)

The Alpine Swap:

- **Zermatt, Switzerland (The Trap):**
  - Avg Hotel: $450/night.
  - Burger & Fries: $35.
- **Theth, Albania (The Dupe):**
  - Guesthouse (incl. 3 meals): $60/night. (**Savings: $390/night**)
  - Experience: Priceless (but actually affordable).

The Carbon Ledger Reality:

Look at those numbers. We are talking about saving thousands of dollars on a single trip.

What could you do with that extra $1,500?

You could work less when you get home.

You could donate it to a local conservation fund in Albania (Insetting).

You could buy better gear that lasts a lifetime.

But more importantly, look at the carbon. Taking the train instead of the plane cuts your emissions by up to 90%. Choosing the Dupe destination often means you are consuming local resources rather than imported ones, slashing your "secondary" footprint.

Conclusion: The Better Story

Ultimately, the European Swap isn't just about saving money or saving carbon. It's about telling a better story.

Do you want to tell the same story as everyone else? *"Yeah, Venice was crowded, the food was expensive, but I got the photo."*

Or do you want to say: *"I stayed in this medieval town called Treviso. I drank Prosecco with an old man named Luigi who taught me how to swear in Italian. I took a ferry to an island in Greece that has no airport, and I listened to the wind for three days straight."*

The Dupe is the better story. It is the story of a Hunter, not a tourist.

Now that we've conquered Europe, let's look at the Tropics. Because if you think the "Greenwashing" is bad in the Alps, wait until you see what they're doing to the beaches in Bali.

Pack your bags. We're going to the jungle.

Chapter 5: The Tropical Swap: Paradise Without the Plastic

Close your eyes. I want you to picture "Paradise."

If you have been alive in the twenty-first century and have access to the internet, I know exactly what you are seeing. You are seeing a white sand beach. The water is that impossible, Gatorade-blue. There is a palm tree leaning at a jaunty forty-five-degree angle. Maybe there is a coconut with a straw in it. Maybe there is a hammock.

It looks peaceful. It looks like the desktop screensaver of the computer you stare at for fifty hours a week. It looks like the answer to every problem you currently have.

Now, open your eyes. Let's talk about the reality.

If you book a ticket to the most famous versions of that picture—Bali, Tulum, Phuket—you are not going to find peace. You are going to find a traffic jam.

You are going to find a beach that is covered in a confetti of microplastics and cigarette butts. You are going to find that the "soothing sound of the ocean" is being drowned out by the thumping bass of a beach club playing generic house music at 2:00 PM. You are going to find that the "local culture" has been paved over to make room for smoothie bowl shacks and stores selling "Live, Laugh, Love" driftwood art.

We have a toxic relationship with the Tropics. We treat these fragile ecosystems like disposable playgrounds. We fly halfway around the world to "connect with nature," and then we demand air conditioning, imported salmon, and plastic-wrapped amenities that destroy the very nature we came to see.

It is the ultimate "Ick."

But the dream isn't dead. The Tropics are still magical, if you know where to look. The heat, the humidity, the smell of damp earth and grilling fish—it hits you in the reptile brain. It makes you feel alive in a way that a cubicle never will.

We just need to stop going to the "Theme Park" versions of paradise. We need to stop chasing the algorithm and start chasing the reality.

This is The Tropical Swap.

We are going to look at three of the biggest offenders in the "Over-Tourism Hall of Fame"—Bali, Tulum, and Costa Rica—and we are going to swap them for destinations that still have their soul intact. We are going to find paradise without the plastic[2].

Part I: The "Eat, Pray, Loathe" Complex

The Trap: Bali

(Traffic, Influencers, and Trash)

Bali was once the "Island of the Gods." Now, it is the Island of the Digital Nomads.

If you go to Canggu or Seminyak today, you are walking into a cautionary tale of unchecked development. The rice paddies are gone, replaced by "Instagram Villas" that all look exactly the same—white concrete, macramé wall hangings, and a pool that takes up 90% of the yard.

The traffic is apocalyptic. I'm not using that word lightly. A three-kilometer drive can take an hour. You are sitting on a scooter, inhaling the exhaust of a thousand other scooters, sweating through your helmet, while a guy with a GoPro strapped to his chest yells at a local family to get out of his way.

And the trash. My god, the trash.

In the rainy season, the beaches of Kuta and Legian are buried under a tide of plastic debris washing in from the ocean and the rivers. It is heartbreaking. You see tourists trying to take selfies, carefully angling their cameras to crop out the pile of diaper wrappers and Coke bottles at their feet. It is a mass delusion.

Bali has become a parody of itself. It is a place where people go to "find themselves," but all they find is other people just like them, paying $15 for avocado toast and talking about their cryptocurrency portfolios. The spirituality has been commodified. You can buy a "chakra alignment" for the price of a used car.

It is crowded. It is noisy. And it is exhausted.

The Dupe: Lombok or Siquijor

(The Way It Used To Be)

You want the rice paddies? You want the surfing? You want the feeling of being on the edge of the world? You have two options that will make you realize just how badly Bali has scammed you.

Option A: Lombok, Indonesia

Look east. Just across the Lombok Strait lies Bali's quieter, wilder sister.

Lombok is what Bali was thirty years ago, before the "Eat, Pray, Love" crowd arrived. The beaches are emptier. The water is clearer. The traffic is non-existent.

The Landscape:

Instead of the crowded Mount Batur sunrise trek (where you are literally standing in a line of 500 people), you have Mount Rinjani. It is a beast of a volcano. It is a serious trek. It demands respect. When you get to the top, you aren't fighting for elbow room; you are fighting for breath, staring down into a crater lake that looks like the eye of God.

The Vibe:

Down south, in Kuta Lombok (not to be confused with the hellhole of Kuta Bali), the roads are wide and flanked by buffalo. The beaches, like Tanjung Aan, are pristine crescents of white sand where the only other people are a few local kids selling coconuts—and they actually chop the coconut open in front of you, they don't serve it to you in a plastic cup with a plastic straw.

You stay in a bamboo bungalow that actually faces the ocean, not a construction site. You eat *Ayam Taliwang* (spicy grilled chicken) that will blow the roof off your mouth, served on a banana leaf, for $2.

Option B: Siquijor, The Philippines

If you want to get even deeper off the grid, go to **Siquijor**.

The Philippines has 7,000 islands, and everyone goes to Palawan or Boracay. Siquijor is the "Mystic Island." For generations, Filipinos were superstitious about it; it was known for shamans, healers, and "aswangs" (witches).

This superstition saved it. It kept the mass developers away.

The Experience:

Siquijor is a mood. You rent a motorbike and drive the circumference of the island in a day. The roads are paved, empty, and wind through jungle canopies that filter the sunlight into neon green beams.

You stop at **Cambugahay Falls**. Yes, it's popular, but it's not "Bali popular." You swing on a vine like Tarzan and drop into turquoise water that is so cold it resets your nervous system.

You go to a *Healer* (Mananambal). Not for a performative Instagram photo, but because that is the culture here. You sit in a wooden shack, smelling burning herbs, and watch a ninety-year-old woman mix potions. Even if you're a cynic—and I am a massive cynic—there is something about Siquijor that vibrates. It feels ancient.

The Trade-Off:

You won't find a Starbucks. You won't find a co-working space with ergonomic chairs. The WiFi will suck.

Good.

You are here to disconnect, remember? Rawdog the silence.

Part II: The "Eco-Chic" Charade

The Trap: Tulum, Mexico

(Generators, Cartels, and $20 Tacos)

Tulum is the ultimate example of "Greenwashing" gone malignant.

Ten years ago, it was a sleepy beach town for hippies. Today, it is a dystopian playground for the rich, disguised as an eco-village.

Everything in Tulum is designed to *look* sustainable. The hotels are made of driftwood and thatch. The restaurants are lit by candlelight. The people are wearing linen and feathers.

But peek behind the curtain.

Tulum is not connected to the power grid. So, how do all those air conditioners and blenders run? **Diesel generators**. Giant, roaring, smog-belching industrial generators are hidden in the jungle behind every "eco-chic" hotel. You are literally breathing diesel fumes while doing yoga, pretending it's *prana*.

And let's talk about the sewage. The infrastructure wasn't built for this many people. I won't get graphic, but let's just say that the beautiful Caribbean water often has a bacterial count that would make a petri dish blush.

Then there is the dark side that nobody puts on the brochure: **The Cartels**.

Where there are rich tourists buying drugs, there is organized crime. The vibe in Tulum has shifted. It is edgy, and not in a cool way. It feels predatory. You are paying New York City prices—$20 for a taco, $25 for a cocktail—to sit in a "beach club" that is effectively privatizing the coastline.

It is expensive. It is fake. It is a theme park for people who want to look like they are burning man, but sleep in 1,000-thread-count sheets.

The Dupe: Bacalar or Puerto Escondido

(The Real Mexico)

You want the water? You want the vibe? Mexico is huge. Stop going to the Riviera Maya and go where the Mexicans go.

Option A: Bacalar (The Lagoon of Seven Colors)

Drive two hours south of Tulum, near the Belize border, and you find **Bacalar**.

This isn't the ocean. It's a freshwater lagoon. And it is, without hyperbole, one of the most beautiful bodies of water on earth. The locals call it the "Lagoon of Seven Colors" because the water shifts from deep indigo to electric turquoise to crystalline clear.

The Win:

Because it is freshwater, there is no Sargassum.

You know that brown, stinky seaweed that is rotting all over the beaches in Tulum and Cancun? That is sargassum. It is a plague caused by ocean warming and fertilizer runoff. It smells like sulfur (rotten eggs) and ruins the beach experience.

Bacalar has none of it.

The Vibe:

Bacalar is sleepy. It is a "Pueblo Mágico" (Magic Town). You stay in a small cabana on the water. You wake up at sunrise—not to beat the crowds, but because the sun rising over the lagoon turns the water into liquid gold, and you don't want to miss it.

You take a sailboat (wind power, not diesel power) to the *Pirates' Canal*. You rub the sulfur-rich sand on your skin—a natural spa treatment that costs zero dollars. You eat *cochinita pibil* tacos from a street stand for 15 pesos, and they taste like history.

Option B: Puerto Escondido (The Surf Capital)

If you need the ocean, swap the Caribbean coast for the Pacific coast. Go to Oaxaca. Go to **Puerto Escondido**.

This is a surf town. Real surf culture, not "surf school" culture. It is gritty, dusty, and unpolished.

The Vibe:

Puerto Escondido is centered around Zicatela Beach, home of the "Mexican Pipeline," one of the deadliest and most famous waves in the world. You don't swim there (unless you want to die), you watch. You sit at a beach bar with a cold Victoria, watching the pros get barreled.

For swimming, you go to **Carrizalillo**, a hidden cove you have to descend 167 steps to reach. The water is calm, the sand is golden, and the vibe is chill.

The Culture:

You are in Oaxaca. The food is superior. We are talking Mole. We are talking Tlayudas (Mexican pizza on a giant tortilla). We are talking Mezcal that tastes like smoke and earth, poured by a bartender who actually likes his job.

Puerto Escondido is growing, yes. But it still feels like a community. It feels like a place where you can walk barefoot down the street and nobody is judging your outfit.

Part III: The "Disneyfication" of Nature

The Trap: Costa Rica

(The American Suburb in the Jungle)

I love Costa Rica. I really do. They have done amazing things for conservation. They abolished their army to fund education. They run on 99% renewable energy.

But let's be real: Costa Rica has become the "Disney" of eco-tourism.

It is the "safe" option. It is where you go if you want to see a monkey but you also want to be 100% sure you can get a burger and fries and speak English the entire time.

In places like Manuel Antonio or La Fortuna, the tourism is industrial-scale. You are shuttled around in air-conditioned vans. You stand in line to walk across a hanging bridge. The "wildlife spotting" often involves twenty people pointing cameras at one depressed sloth that is trying to sleep.

And the prices? You are paying American prices. A simple meal (*casado*) can cost $15-$20 in tourist zones. The entry fees for national parks are steep. It feels curated. It feels sanitized. It feels like "Adventure Lite."

The Dupe: Panama

(The Wild West)

Cross the border to the south, and everything changes.

Panama has the same biodiversity as Costa Rica. The same jungles. The same oceans (Caribbean and Pacific). The same sloths, toucans, and jaguars.

But it has a fraction of the tourists.

The Vibe:

Panama feels wilder. It feels unpolished. The infrastructure isn't perfect—the roads can be potholed, the buses are chaotic—but that is the point. You are in Central America, not a theme park.

The Locations:

- **Bocas del Toro:** This is your Caribbean fix. It's an archipelago of islands near the Costa Rican border. It has a raucous, pirate-island energy. You take water taxis between islands. You snorkel in **Starfish Beach**, where the bottom is literally carpeted with giant orange starfish. It's rough around the edges, partying at night, but pure magic by day.

- Santa Catalina / Coiba National Park: This is the Pacific side. Coiba is often called the "Galapagos of Panama." It's a former island prison (like Alcatraz) that is now a UNESCO heritage site. Because it was a prison, nobody lived there for a century. The nature took over.

You dive here, and you are surrounded by sharks, rays, turtles, and whales. It is primal. It makes the snorkeling in Costa Rica look like a goldfish bowl.

The Cost:

Panama uses the US Dollar, so you don't get a currency exchange arbitrage, but the prices are lower. You can get a fresh ceviche in Panama City's fish market for $3. You can stay in a hostel in lush mountain towns like Boquete for cheap.

The Edge:

Panama has the Darién Gap. We aren't suggesting you go there (seriously, don't, it's dangerous). But just knowing it's there—that untamed, impassable jungle separating the continents—gives the whole country a feeling of being on the frontier. Costa Rica feels conquered. Panama feels like it's still negotiating with the jungle.

Part IV: The Reef-Safe Reality

(Chemical Warfare on the Ocean)

We need to have a serious conversation about what you are putting on your skin.

You are a Dupe Hunter. You've avoided the trap. You've found the pristine beach in Siquijor or Bacalar. The water is crystal clear. You strip down, slather yourself in sunscreen, and jump in.

You just committed a chemical attack.

Most standard sunscreens—the stuff you buy at the drugstore—contain **Oxybenzone** and **Octinoxate**. These are chemicals that absorb UV light. They are great for preventing sunburn. They are catastrophic for coral reefs.

When these chemicals wash off your skin (and they do, instantly), they act as an endocrine disruptor for coral. They bleach it. They damage its DNA. They effectively sterilize the reef so it cannot reproduce.

A single drop of Oxybenzone in an Olympic-sized swimming pool is enough to be toxic to coral. Now imagine 5,000 tourists a day, all marinating in the stuff, jumping into a bay. It is a slow-motion oil spill.

The Solution: Mineral Only

You need to switch to **Mineral Sunscreen**. Look for **Zinc Oxide** or **Titanium Dioxide** as the active ingredients.

- *How to tell the difference:* Chemical sunscreen rubs in invisible. Mineral sunscreen leaves a bit of a white cast (the "Mark Zuckerberg on a surfboard" look).

- *The Hack:* Embrace the white cast. It's a badge of honor. It says, "I am not killing this reef." Or, get a tinted mineral sunscreen that matches your skin tone.

- *Better yet:* Wear a rash guard (swim shirt). It covers 90% of your upper body, so you don't need sunscreen there at all. It never washes off. It never expires. It is the ultimate eco-gear.

The Plastic Plagues

(Leave No Trace 2.0)

In the tropics, there is no "away."

When you throw a plastic bottle in a bin on a small island, where do you think it goes? There are no recycling plants. It goes into a landfill behind the village, where it will eventually blow into the ocean, or it gets burned, releasing toxic fumes into the air you are breathing.

The Dupe Hunter follows a stricter code:

1. **Bring the Filter Bottle:** We mentioned this in the gear guide, but in the tropics, it is non-negotiable. If you buy three plastic bottles of water a day for two weeks, that is 42 bottles. If you use a filter bottle, that is zero.

2. **Refuse the Straw:** "No straw, please" (*Sin popote, por favor* in Spanish). Learn this phrase. Tattoo it on your arm.

3. **Pack It Out:** If you use a solid shampoo bar or a razor, take the trash home with you. Your home country probably has a waste management system. The island doesn't. Be a mule for your own waste.

Conclusion: The "Paradise" Paradox

The tropics are seductive. They promise us a return to Eden. But we have to remember that Eden didn't have Wi-Fi, air conditioning, or infinity pools. When we demand 5-Star luxury in the middle of a jungle, we are demanding the destruction of the jungle. We are demanding that the environment be bent to our will.

The "Dupe Hunter" approach is about bending *our* will to the environment.

It is about accepting that paradise might be a little sweatier, a little dustier, and a little harder to get to. It implies that the best beach isn't the one with the butler service; it's the one where you are the only person leaving footprints.

We swap the plastic for the authentic. We swap the generator hum for the sound of cicadas. We swap the convenience for the connection.

And trust me, when you are floating in the freshwater of Bacalar, watching the sunrise without a single influencer in sight, you won't miss the butler.

Now, dry off. We need to talk about what happens on the flight home. Or rather, what happens *during* the flight. Put your phone away. We are going to learn how to **Rawdog** the journey. Turn the page to Chapter 6.

Chapter 6: The "Rawdog" Rebellion: Silent Travel & Digital Detox

Let's talk about the most terrifying thing you can possibly do in the modern world.

It isn't swimming with sharks. It isn't solo hiking in the Albanian Alps. It isn't eating street meat in a place where the health code is "don't die."

The most terrifying thing you can do is sit alone in a room, with no phone, no television, no book, no music, and no distraction, and just *be* there.

If the thought of that makes your chest tight, you are not alone. We are a civilization of addicts. We are addicted to input. We are addicted to the little red notification badge. We are addicted to the feeling of being "connected," even though we all know, deep down in our dopamine-fried brains, that scrolling through the vacation photos of a girl you went to high school with fifteen years ago isn't connection. It's anesthetic.

We use noise to drown out the silence. Because in the silence, you have to hear your own thoughts. And for most of us, those thoughts are a chaotic mix of anxiety, to-do lists, and the creeping suspicion that we are wasting our lives.

So, we travel. We fly to the other side of the world to "get away from it all."

But what do we do the second we land? We turn on roaming. We hunt for Wi-Fi passwords like they are oxygen. We curate the experience for an audience back home before we have even processed it ourselves. We aren't seeing the Taj Mahal; we are seeing a screen that is showing us the Taj Mahal.

We are physically in paradise, but mentally, we are still in the inbox.

This chapter is about breaking that cycle. It is about the **"Rawdog" Rebellion**. It is about the radical, counter-cultural act of shutting up, turning off, and facing the world naked.

Part I: The Flight of the Rawdog

The Trend That Scared the Boomers

In late 2024 and early 2025, a trend emerged on TikTok that confused the hell out of the older generations. It was called **"Rawdogging" a flight**.

The premise was simple: You get on a long-haul flight - seven hours, ten hours, maybe even London to Sydney. And you do... nothing.

No movies. No noise-canceling headphones playing a podcast. No sleeping pills. No book. No Wi-Fi.

You just sit there. You stare at the seat-back map. You watch the little plane icon inch across the blue digital ocean. You eat the rubbery chicken when it comes. You drink the water. You think.

The media called it "psychotic." They called it "torture."

But they missed the point. It wasn't torture. It was a **Dopamine Detox**.

We are living in an era of over-stimulation. Our brains are being fire-hosed with information every waking second. We have forgotten how to be bored. And because we have forgotten how to be bored, we have forgotten how to think.

The "Rawdog" trend wasn't about suffering; it was about resilience. It was a flex. It was Gen Z looking at the attention economy and saying: *"You don't own me. I can sit with my own thoughts for twelve hours and not crumble."*

The Physics of Boredom

Here is what happens when you rawdog a flight (or a train ride, or a bus trip).

Hour 1: You are fidgety. You reach for your phone, realize it's off, and feel a phantom limb twitch. You look around the cabin. You judge the guy in 14C for taking his shoes off.

Hour 3: The boredom sets in. It hurts. It feels physical, like an itch behind your eyes. Your brain is screaming for a hit of dopamine. It wants a cat video. It wants a headline. It wants *sugar*.

Hour 5: The fever breaks.

Something shifts. The itch stops. Your brain, realizing that no stimulation is coming, stops fighting and starts drifting. You enter a state that neuroscientists call the "Default Mode Network." This is where creativity lives. This is where problem-solving lives.

Suddenly, you aren't just enduring the flight. You are thinking about your life with a clarity you haven't had in years. You are processing that breakup. You are realizing you hate your job. You are remembering the smell of your grandmother's kitchen.

By the time you land, you aren't exhausted. You are reset.

Travel is supposed to be a portal. It is supposed to take you from one state of being to another. But if you spend the entire transition distracted by the same movies you could watch on your couch, you aren't traveling. You are just teleporting your body while your mind stays in Hollywood.

The Action Step:

On your next trip, try it. Maybe not the full twelve hours if you aren't ready. But try the first two.

Keep the headphones off during takeoff. Listen to the engines. Watch the ground fall away. Look at the clouds.

Reclaim your attention span. It is the most valuable currency you have.

Part II: Silence is the New Luxury

The Noise Pollution Crisis

We talk a lot about air pollution and plastic pollution. We rarely talk about **Noise Pollution**.

But if you live in a city, you are bathing in it. The hum of traffic, the sirens, the construction, the HVAC systems, the ding of elevators. It is a constant, low-level assault on your nervous system.

Your body interprets loud noise as a threat. It spikes your cortisol. It keeps you in "fight or flight" mode, even when you are just buying a latte.

This is why **"Silence"** has become the ultimate status symbol.

Go to a budget hotel. The walls are paper-thin. You can hear the TV next door, the elevator dinging, the traffic outside.

Go to a 5-Star ultra-luxury resort. What are you paying for? You are paying for thick walls. You are paying for a private villa set back from the road. You are paying for the absence of noise.

The "Dupe Hunter" knows this. But the Dupe Hunter also knows that you don't need to pay $2,000 a night to find silence. You just need to go where the noise isn't.

The "Coolcation" Connection

We mentioned "Coolcations" (seeking temperate climates to escape the heat) earlier[4]. There is a huge overlap here.

Heat creates noise. Hot places are loud - air conditioners roaring, people outside late at night, crowded beaches.

Cold places are quiet. Snow absorbs sound. Mist dampens acoustics.

There is a specific kind of silence you find in the Scottish Highlands or the fjords of Norway or the mountains of Patagonia. It is a heavy, blanketed silence. It forces you to slow down.

This is the **"Silent Travel"** trend. It is the conscious decision to choose destinations based on their acoustic profile. It is seeking out the "sonic dupes" - places where the soundtrack is wind and water, not combustion and conversation.

Part III: The Destinations

Where to Find the Void

So, where do we go to find this silence? We aren't looking for a sensory deprivation tank. We are looking for places that demand our full attention.

1. Dark Sky Parks

(The Visual Silence)

Light pollution is just noise for your eyes.

Most of us have never seen the sky. Not really. We see a hazy, orange soup with a few bright dots that might be stars or might be satellites.

A **International Dark Sky Park** is a protected area with zero light pollution[6]. It is the "Dupe" for space travel.

The Experience:

You go to a place like Aoraki Mackenzie in New Zealand, or Cherry Springs State Park in Pennsylvania, or Westhavelland in Germany.

You drive in. You turn off your headlights. And you look up.

It is violent. That is the only word for it. The Milky Way isn't a smudge; it is a rip in the fabric of the sky. You see thousands - literally thousands - of stars. You feel the curvature of the earth.

This triggers a feeling called **"The Overview Effect"** (usually reserved for astronauts). It is a mix of awe and existential terror. You realize how small you are. You realize that your emails, your anxieties, and your credit score are completely irrelevant in the face of this cosmic machinery.

That feeling? That is the ultimate reset. It puts your ego in a blender.

The Dupe Strategy:

You don't need a telescope. You just need a blanket and patience.

- **The Trap:** Going to a city observatory or a planetarium. (Fake, projected, crowded).
- **The Dupe:** Driving two hours into the desert or the mountains to a designated Dark Sky zone. (Real, free, life-changing).

2. The Monastery Stay

(The Spiritual Dupe)

Let's talk about "Wellness Retreats."

You know the ones. They are in Malibu or Bali. They cost $5,000 for a weekend. You wear white robes. You drink green juice. You talk about your "journey."

Most of these are scams. They are luxury hotels with a spiritual veneer.

If you want the real thing - if you want to confront your demons and find actual peace - you go to a **Monastery**.

The Dupe:

Monasteries (Buddhist, Catholic, Orthodox) have been doing "wellness" for two thousand years. They don't call it wellness. They call it discipline.

Many monasteries accept guests for a nominal fee or a donation (often $40-$50 a night).

The Experience:

This is not a spa. The bed will be hard. The food will be simple (soup, bread, vegetables). The wake-up call will be a bell at 4:30 AM.

And in many of them, there is a vow of silence.

- **Mount Athos (Greece):** (Note: Men only, unfortunately). Time stopped here in the Byzantine era. No cars, no electricity in many parts, just chanting and the sea.
- **Koyasan (Japan):** You stay in a temple (*Shukubo*). You eat *Shojin Ryori* (monk's vegan cuisine). You meditate in a cemetery surrounded by giant cedar trees.

- **Plum Village (France):** Thich Nhat Hanh's monastery. It's accessible, modern, but deeply rooted in mindfulness.

Why it works:

In a $5,000 retreat, the staff is paid to be nice to you. They cater to your ego.

In a monastery, the monks don't care about your ego. You are there to work. You sweep the courtyard. You wash your bowl. You sit in silence.

It strips away the pretension. You realize that "wellness" isn't something you buy; it's something you do.

3. The Silent Retreat (Vipassana)

(The Nuclear Option)

If you really want to "Rawdog" your existence, sign up for a **Vipassana** retreat.

Ten days. No talking. No reading. No writing. No eye contact. No phone. Just you and your breath for ten hours a day.

It is free. (Donation based). It is found all over the world.

I will be honest with you: The first three days are hell. Your brain will scream. You will replay every embarrassing moment of your life. You will hallucinate the sound of your ringtone. You will hate everyone in the room.

But by day four, the noise stops. The silt settles in the glass. You start to see things as they are, not as you fear them to be.

This is the ultimate "Dupe Hunter" move. It costs nothing but time and courage. And you come out of it with a mind that is sharper than a diamond.

Part IV: The Digital Boundary

How to Travel With a Phone But Live Without It

Okay, let's get practical.

Maybe you aren't ready for a monastery. Maybe you just want to go to Italy and not spend the whole time on Instagram.

The problem is that the smartphone is a Swiss Army Knife. It is your map, your boarding pass, your translator, your currency converter, and your camera. You *can't* leave it at home.

So, how do we build a wall between the "Tool" functions and the "Trap" functions?

We need to set a **Digital Boundary**.

1. The "Dumb Phone" Simulation

You don't need to buy a burner phone. You just need to lobotomize your iPhone.

- **Delete the Apps:** Before you leave for the airport, delete Instagram, TikTok, Twitter/X, LinkedIn, and email.
  - *The Panic:* "But what if I need to post a story?" You don't.
  - *The Reality:* You can re-download them when you get home. By deleting them, you remove the muscle memory twitch. When you unlock your phone to check Google Maps, you won't accidentally drift into scrolling.
- **Grayscale Mode:**
  - This is the best hack in existence. Go into your accessibility settings and turn your screen black and white.
  - Suddenly, your phone looks like a newspaper. The red badges don't pop. The Instagram photos look dull.
  - Your brain loses interest. You check the map, and you put it away. You turn your phone back into a tool, not a toy.

2. The "Camera" Paradox

We have a sickness where we believe that if we didn't take a picture of it, it didn't happen.

We see a sunset, and our first instinct is to capture it, compress it, and store it.

But there is a cost. When you look at a sunset through a screen, you aren't seeing the sunset. You are seeing a digital representation of it. You are stepping out of the moment to document the moment.

The "One Shot" Rule:

Treat your phone like it has film. Give yourself permission to take one photo of the monument. Make it count. Compose it. Click it.

Then put the phone away.

Stare at the thing for five minutes. Burn it into your actual retina.

3. The "No-Phone" Zone

Designate "No-Phone" times or zones during your trip.

- **Meals:** Never, ever have your phone on the table. Not even face down. Leave it in the hotel room, or deep in your bag. Taste the food. Talk to your companion. Watch the other diners.

- **The Bedroom:** Do not charge your phone next to the bed. Charge it in the bathroom. Buy a cheap analog alarm clock if you need one.

    - If the last thing you see before you sleep is blue light and work emails, you aren't resting. You are marinating in stress.

    - If the first thing you see when you wake up is a notification, you have already lost the day.

Part V: Workbook Element: The Sensory Log

Replacing Consumption with Absorption

We are visual gluttons. We consume travel with our eyes, but we starve our other senses.

Instagram has ruined travel because it has flattened the world into a 1080x1350 pixel rectangle. We go to places that "look good."

But the best travel experiences often look like nothing.

The smell of burning peat in Ireland.

The sticky humidity of a Bangkok night market.

The sound of church bells echoing off stone in a Croatian alley.

The taste of a tomato that actually has flavor.

You can't photograph these things. You have to feel them.

Instead of a "Photo Dump," I want you to keep a **Sensory Log**.

This is a physical notebook. Not a notes app. A notebook.

The Exercise:

Once a day, sit down for ten minutes. Maybe with a coffee, maybe with a beer. Write down one thing for each sense.

- **Sight:** (Don't just describe the view. Look for the detail. The way the light hit the dust motes. The specific shade of blue on the fisherman's boat).

- **Sound:** (The "Soundscape." Is it the roar of a Vespa? The chirping of cicadas? The specific rhythm of the language being spoken?)

- **Smell:** (This is the strongest link to memory. Does the city smell like diesel and jasmine? Does the ocean smell like salt and decay? Does the bakery smell like yeast?)

- **Taste:** (The acidity of the wine. The spice of the curry. The sweetness of the fruit).

- **Touch:** (The cobblestones under your feet. The coolness of the linen sheet. The heat of the sun on your neck).

Why do this?

Two reasons.

1. **It forces you to pay attention.** You can't write about the smell if you haven't sniffed the air. You become a hunter of sensation.

2. **It builds a better memory.** Five years from now, that photo of the sunset will just be a photo. But if you read your note about the smell of the charcoal smoke and the sound of the old man laughing, you will be instantly transported back.

Sample Entry:

- *Location:* Hanoi, Vietnam.

- *Sound:* A constant river of honking, but friendly honking. The hiss of oil in a wok.

- *Smell:* Fish sauce, exhaust, and wet pavement.

- *Taste:* The broth is salty, sour, and incredibly deep. Coffee with condensed milksugar shock.

- *Touch:* The plastic stool is digging into my legs. The air is heavy, like wearing a wet blanket.

- *Sight:* A woman carrying a mountain of flowers on a bicycle.

That is better than a selfie. That is reality.

Conclusion: The Rebellion

We called this chapter "The Rawdog Rebellion" because that is what it is.

In an economy that is designed to harvest your attention, keeping your attention for yourself is a revolutionary act.

In a world that screams, silence is a weapon.

When you travel in silence - when you turn off the podcast, put away the phone, and just sit with the world - you are doing something radical. You are refusing to be a spectator.

You are refusing to let an algorithm mediate your experience of reality.

You are refusing to numb yourself to the boredom, the awkwardness, and the beauty.

You are showing up. Naked. Vulnerable. Awake.

And that, my friends, is the only way to actually see the world.

Now that we have cleared your head, let's get moving. We've sat still long enough. It's time to talk about the journey itself. It's time to stop flying and start rolling.

Turn the page. We're going to talk about trains.

The "Vipassana" Panic Attack

I walked into the Vipassana center with the swagger of a person who has completely underestimated the enemy.

I thought I was ready. I thought, "Hey, I'm an introvert. I hate small talk. I love napping. Ten days of silence? This is going to be a vacation." I imagined myself floating in a pool of serenity, finally having the time to think deep, profound thoughts about the universe, untethered from the tyranny of my inbox. I handed over my iPhone to the course manager at the registration desk with a flourish, like a cowboy holstering his gun. "Take it," I thought. "I don't need it. I am above technology."

I was an arrogant fool.

By Day 2, I was plotting a prison break.

If you have never done a Vipassana retreat, you need to understand the rules. It is not just "no talking." It is "Noble Silence." No gestures. No eye contact. No reading. No writing. No exercise. Just you, a cushion, and the screaming chaotic mess that is your own mind, for ten hours a day.

The panic didn't hit immediately. The first few hours were novel. It felt like a game. But then the sun went down, and the withdrawal set in.

It turns out, I am not addicted to my phone because I love my phone. I am addicted to my phone because I hate being bored. And without the digital pacifier, boredom in a silent meditation hall becomes a physical sensation. It felt like ants crawling under my skin. My brain, starved of its usual diet of dopamine hits, headlines, and cat videos, started to cannibalize itself.

I sat on my blue cushion in the Dhamma Hall, surrounded by eighty other silent people. And I began to lose my mind.

The enemy was not the silence. The enemy was the guy sitting three rows in front of me. Let's call him "The Sniffler."

Every forty-five seconds—I counted—he would inhale sharply through his nose. *Sniff.* Then a pause. Then a wet, gurgling swallow. *Gulp.*

In the real world, I would have put on headphones. I would have walked away. But here, I was trapped. I was a prisoner of his sinuses. The sound became the only thing in the universe. It grew louder and louder until it sounded like a jet engine. I started having violent fantasies involving duct tape and a very steep cliff. I spent three hours of "meditation" not focusing on my breath, but mentally composing a scathing letter to the management about nasal hygiene, which I couldn't write down because I didn't have a pen.

By the afternoon of Day 3, the physical pain set in. We sit cross-legged. Humans are not designed to sit cross-legged for ten hours a day. My knees felt like they were being drilled with hot pokers. My back was a knot of agony.

And then came the phantom vibrations.

I swear to you, I felt my phone buzzing in my pocket. I reached down to check it, panic flaring in my chest—*Did I miss an email? Is there an emergency?*—only to grab a handful of sweatpants. My phone was locked in a safe in the office. But my thigh nerves were so conditioned to the dopamine trigger that they were firing on their own. I was twitching like a junkie in rehab.

This was the panic attack.

It happened during the 4:00 PM sitting of strong determination (*Adhiṭṭhāna*). You aren't supposed to move for an hour.

My brain started screaming. It was a cacophony of every insecurity I had ever suppressed. *You're wasting your life. You're bad at your job. Remember that time in 7th grade you called the teacher 'Mom'? Everyone hates you. Why are you sitting here? You could be eating pizza. You could be watching Netflix. GET OUT.*

My heart hammered against my ribs. I couldn't breathe. The silence of the room felt heavy, like it was crushing me. I wanted to stand up and scream. I wanted to run out the door, hijack a car, and drive until I found a Starbucks. I wanted noise. I wanted distraction. I wanted to numb the feeling of being just *me*.

I realized then that I had spent the last ten years of my life running away from this exact feeling. I had filled every quiet moment with a podcast, every waiting room with a scroll, every toilet break with a game. I had terrified myself with the prospect of my own company.

I sat there, sweating, tears leaking out of my eyes, convinced I was dying.

And then, the bell rang.

The hour was over. I hadn't died. I hadn't screamed. The Sniffler sniffed one last time, and we all stood up and shuffled out to tea.

The break didn't happen until Day 6.

I was walking in the small garden allotment we were allowed to use. I was looking at a tree. Just a regular, scrubby pine tree. I had walked past it fifty times.

But this time, I saw it. I saw the way the bark peeled back in rough, geometric scales. I saw a line of ants marching up the trunk, carrying tiny white crumbs. I saw the way the light hit the needles, turning them from forest green to gold.

I stopped. My brain was quiet. The Sniffler didn't matter. The phantom buzzing was gone. The narrative loop of my insecurities had finally run out of battery.

For the first time in a decade, I wasn't thinking about the next thing. I wasn't curating the moment for an audience. I wasn't worrying about an email. I was just looking at a tree.

It was the most high-definition experience of my life. The colors were saturated. The air tasted sweet. The silence wasn't empty anymore; it was full. It was heavy with presence.

I realized that the "Rawdog" rebellion isn't about punishing yourself. It isn't about being a masochist. It's about cleaning the windshield. We drive through life with a windshield covered in mud and dead bugs—distractions, notifications, anxieties. We think the world is blurry and gray.

But when you finally wipe it clean—when you endure the panic and get to the other side—you realize the world is bright. It is sharp. It is agonizingly beautiful.

I left the center four days later. They gave me back my phone. I held it in my hand. It felt heavy. It felt like a loaded weapon.

I turned it on. The notifications flooded in. 142 emails. 36 texts. 15 Instagram alerts.

I looked at them. I felt a twinge of the old anxiety, the old "feed me" impulse. But it was fainter now. I knew what it was. It wasn't connection. It was just noise.

I put the phone in my pocket. I didn't check the emails. I walked outside, took a deep breath of the real air, and listened to the sound of my own footsteps.

I was back in the world. But for the first time, I was actually *in* it.

Chapter 7: Train Bragging (Tagskryt): Making the Journey the Flex

Let's be honest about the modern airport experience.

It is a humiliation ritual.

You arrive three hours early. You stand in a line that snakes back and forth like a labyrinth designed by a sadist. You take off your shoes. You take off your belt. You hold your pants up with one hand while you put your laptop in a plastic bin that has been touched by ten thousand other unwashed hands. You walk through a scanner that shows a stranger the outline of your junk. You get yelled at for having 101 milliliters of shampoo.

Then, you walk into a holding pen that smells like Cinnabon and anxiety. You pay $14 for a sandwich wrapped in plastic that tastes like wet cardboard. You sit at the gate, fighting for an outlet to charge your phone, waiting for a delay announcement.

Finally, you get on the metal tube. You wedge your knees into the seat in front of you. The air is recycled. The person next to you is coughing. For the next four hours, you are not a human being; you are cargo. You are a biological package being shipped from Point A to Point B, and the airline would very much prefer it if you would just go into suspended animation so they didn't have to give you a half-can of ginger ale.

We have convinced ourselves that this is "luxury" because we get some frequent flyer miles. We have convinced ourselves that this is "efficient" because the flight time is only two hours (ignoring the four hours of purgatory on either side).

But the vibe has shifted. The "Jet Set" era is dead. Flying isn't a flex anymore. It's a chore. It's a Greyhound bus in the sky, but with more security theater and a higher carbon footprint.

There is a new status symbol in town. It comes from Sweden (of course it does). It is called ***Tagskryt***.

Translation: **Train Bragging**.

In 2025, the flex isn't posting a photo of your boarding pass to Dubai. The flex is posting a photo of your legs stretched out in a train cabin, a bottle of wine on the table, watching the Swiss Alps or the Italian coast blur past the window.

The flex is showing the world that you have time. That you have taste. That you are smart enough to opt out of the misery of the airport and into the romance of the rails.

This chapter is about reclaiming the journey. It is about understanding that how you get there matters just as much as where you are going. It is about reframing the "lost time" of travel into "gained time" for your life.

Part I: The Mindset Shift

Reframing the "Lost Time"

We are obsessed with speed. We wear "busy" like a badge of honor. If you tell someone you are taking a train that takes six hours instead of a flight that takes one hour, they look at you like you just announced you are churning your own butter.

"Six hours? Who has time for that?"

You do. And here is why the math is wrong.

Let's look at the **Door-to-Door Reality**.

The Flight:

- Travel to airport (remote location): 60 mins.
- Security/Check-in buffer: 120 mins.
- Flight time: 90 mins.
- Taxiing/Deplaning: 30 mins.
- Travel from airport to city center: 60 mins.
- **Total Time:** 6 hours.
- **Quality of Time:** Zero. You are stressed, moving, queuing, and disconnected. You cannot work. You cannot relax. You are in "transit mode."

The Train:

- Travel to station (city center): 20 mins.
- Buffer: 15 mins. (You walk on).
- Train time: 5 hours.
- Arrival (city center): 0 mins.
- **Total Time:** ~5.5 hours.
- **Quality of Time:** High.

This is the Manson-style reality check: **You aren't losing time; you are gaining autonomy.**

On the train, you have a table. You have Wi-Fi (usually). You can walk around. You can go to the bar. You can read a book. You can write the Great American Novel.

When you are on a train, nobody expects you to be anywhere else. It is a hall pass from the obligations of life. It is "Gained Time". It is a mobile office, a mobile dining room, and a mobile bedroom.

The *Tagskryt* mindset creates a shift in how you value yourself. The tourist rushes because they are desperate to consume the destination. The traveler lingers because they understand that the movement itself is the destination.

The Bourdain Factor: The Dining Car

There is something inherently civilized about a dining car.

I'm not talking about the plastic tray table on a Boeing 737 where you peel the foil off a container of pasta that is simultaneously boiling hot and frozen in the middle.

I'm talking about a white tablecloth. Heavy cutlery. A glass of Riesling that catches the light as the train banks around a curve.

In the dining car of a European train, you are forced to be human. You might be seated across from a stranger. In an airplane, the goal is to build an invisible wall between you and your neighbor. On a train, the goal is to break bread.

You eat a Schnitzel on the Austrian Railjet. You drink a coffee on the Italian Frecciarossa. You watch the world change. The architecture shifts from Germanic timber to Italian stucco. The light changes from cool blue to warm gold. You are digesting the geography along with your meal.

This is the "Flex." It isn't about how much money you spent. It's about the fact that while your friends are currently taking their shoes off for a TSA agent in Newark, you are eating a croissant in the south of France.

Part II: 5 Epic Rail Journeys

The Routes That Beat Flying

You want to start *Tagskryt-ing*? You need the right ammunition. You need routes that are faster, cheaper, or simply infinitely better than the flight.

Here are five epic rail journeys that prove the point.

1. The Gateway Drug: London to Amsterdam (Eurostar)

This is the route that converts the skeptics.

London to Amsterdam is one of the busiest flight routes in Europe. It is also miserable. Heathrow is a city-sized panic attack. Schiphol is a labyrinth.

The Train Flex:

You walk into St. Pancras International in London. It is a cathedral of brick and glass. You grab a coffee. You breeze through a simplified security check.

You board the Eurostar. You settle into a wide seat.

The train slips out of London, dives into a tunnel under the English Channel (an engineering miracle we take for granted), and pops out in France. Then Belgium. Then the Netherlands.

The Stats:

- **Time:** 3 hours and 52 minutes.
- **The Win:** You arrive at Amsterdam Centraal, literally in the heart of the city. You step off the train and you are looking at canals.
- **The Brag:** Posting a video of your speedometer hitting 300km/h (186mph) while your beer doesn't even ripple.

2. The Romantic: The Nightjet (Vienna to Venice)

We will talk more about night trains later, but this is the crown jewel. This is the route that makes you feel like you are in a Wes Anderson movie.

The Train Flex:

You board the ÖBB Nightjet in Vienna in the evening. You have a private sleeper cabin (if you booked early) or a couchette. It's compact, clever, and cozy.

You go to the dining car. You have a glass of Austrian wine. You sleep while the train winds through the Austrian Alps.

The Awakening:

This is the moment. You wake up. You lift the blind.

You are crossing the lagoon. The water is flat and silver in the morning light. The bell towers of Venice are rising out of the mist.

You roll into Venezia Santa Lucia station. You walk out the front doors and—boom—the Grand Canal is right there. No water taxi from the airport. No bus. You are there.

The Brag: "I went to sleep in Austria and woke up in Italy. Total cost of transport: less than a hotel room."

3. The Scenic Mic Drop: The Bernina Express (Chur to Tirano)

This is not about speed. This is about spectacle. This is the train ride that makes Instagram filters obsolete.

Connecting Switzerland and Italy, the Bernina Express is the highest railway across the Alps. It doesn't use cogwheels; it just powers its way up the mountain through sheer Swiss engineering determination.

The Train Flex:

The windows are panoramic. They curve into the roof.

You pass glaciers. You pass frozen lakes. You spiral through the Brusio Circular Viaduct—a 360-degree loop that looks like a toy train set come to life.

You go from the snowy, disciplined silence of the Swiss Alps to the palm trees and chaotic warmth of Italy in four hours.

The Brag: A photo of the red train against the white snow. Caption: "Your window seat looks at a wing. My window seat looks at a glacier."

4. The Gritty Adventure: The Reunification Express (Hanoi to Da Nang)

Let's leave Europe for a second. Let's go to Vietnam.

The "Reunification Express" (officially the North-South Railway) runs the length of the country. But the section from Hanoi to Da Nang (specifically the Hai Van Pass) is legendary.

The Train Flex:

This is Bourdain country. The train is older. It rattles. It smells of diesel and instant noodles. It is real.

As you hit the Hai Van Pass, the train clings to the edge of the cliff. On one side, the jungle rises vertically. On the other side, a sheer drop to the South China Sea (East Sea).

You lean out the window (yes, you can often open them). The humid air hits you. You buy a boiled egg and a beer from a lady pushing a cart. You are moving through the landscape, not over it.

The Brag: "Woke up in the jungle. Lunch by the ocean. Dinner in the Imperial City. No turbulence, just vibes."

5. The American Dream: The Coast Starlight (Seattle to Los Angeles)

Americans, you are not excluded from this. You have one of the most beautiful train routes on earth, even if you refuse to fund it properly.

The Train Flex:

The Coast Starlight runs down the West Coast. The section south of San Luis Obispo is magic. The tracks are literally on the beach. You are closer to the ocean than Highway 1.

You sit in the Observation Car—a lounge with floor-to-ceiling windows and swivel chairs. You watch the Pacific Ocean crash against the rocks. You see surfers. You see whales.

The Brag: "Why drive I-5 and stare at bumper stickers when I can drink a gin and tonic and stare at the Pacific?"

Part III: The Night Train Renaissance

Sleeping Your Way to Savings

There is a specific economic hack that the Dupe Hunter loves: **The Night Train.**

It is the ultimate efficiency. You are combining your transportation and your accommodation into one ticket.

Let’s say a hotel in Paris costs $200. A flight from Berlin to Paris costs $100. Total: $300 (plus the misery of the airport).

A sleeper cabin on the Nightjet might cost $150.

You just saved $150, and you didn't lose a day to travel. You teleported in your sleep.

This is the **Night Train Renaissance**. After years of decline, Europe is bringing them back. New routes are opening up every month. Zurich to Barcelona. Brussels to Prague.

The Reality Check (Manson Style):

I’m not going to lie to you. Sleeping on a train is not sleeping at the Ritz.

- It shakes.
- It makes noise.
- The bathroom is down the hall (unless you pay for the deluxe cabin).
- You might have roommates if you book a couchette (bunk bed style).

But that is part of the adventure. It is intimate. It is communal.

The Strategy:

1. **Bring Earplugs:** Essential. Good silicone ones.
2. **Bring an Eye Mask:** The station lights can be bright.
3. **Book Early:** Night trains are popular. The private cabins sell out weeks in advance.
4. **The "Couchette" Life:** If you are on a budget, book a couchette (4 or 6 beds). It’s like a hostel on wheels. You meet people. You share snacks. It’s a story.

Part IV: The Man in Seat 61

Your Guide to the Rails

If this book is your bible, then **Mark Smith** is your prophet.

Mark Smith is the guy who runs **The Man in Seat 61** (seat61.com).

This website looks like it was built in 2005. It has no fancy animations. It has no influencer photos.

And it is the single most valuable travel resource on the internet.

Mark Smith has ridden every train. He explains how to buy tickets when the foreign websites reject your credit card. He tells you which side of the train has the best view. He tells you what the coffee tastes like.

How to Use It:

Do not use generic booking sites like "RailEurope" or "Omio" as your first stop. They charge fees and don't show all the routes.

1. Go to Seat61.com.

2. Click on your starting country (e.g., "London to...").

3. Click on your destination (e.g., "...Italy").

4. Read. He will give you the exact "Option 1," "Option 2," and "Option 3."

5. Follow his links to the *official* operator sites (SNCF, Trenitalia, DB) to book direct and save money.

The Action Step:

Before you book any flight within Europe (or Asia), check Seat 61. Just look. If the train is under 6 hours, take the train. If it's under 12 hours, check for a night train.

Part V: The Social Flex

The Anti-Pod

There is a final reason to brag about the train. It's the people.

Air travel is designed to be anti-social. We put on noise-canceling headphones. We stare at screens. We are terrified of the person next to us initiating a conversation.

Train travel is different. The seating arrangements (often face-to-face with a table) encourage interaction. The pacing allows for it.

I have shared a bottle of wine with a grandmother in Portugal who didn't speak a word of English but taught me how to eat sardines properly.

I have argued about politics with a student in Germany.

I have played cards with a family in Thailand.

These aren't "transactions." They are connections.

In a world where we are increasingly isolated in our digital silos, the train forces us to physically share space with the rest of humanity. It reminds us that we are part of a society.

And that? That is the biggest flex of all.

The Conclusion: Trains & Plans

The plane is about leaving. The train is about arriving.

The plane is a capsule. The train is a thread that stitches the landscape together.

So, next time you are planning a trip, don't just default to the "Sky Bus." Look at the rails. Be the person who rolls into the city center, rested, fed, and full of stories, while your friends are still waiting for their bags at Carousel 4.

Tagskryt. Wear it proud.

Now that you know how to move, let's talk about how to stop. Let's talk about staying in one place and going deep. Turn the page to **The Slowmad Protocol**.

The Night Train Confessional

The first rule of air travel is isolation. You put on your noise-canceling headphones before the safety demonstration even starts. You erect a psychic force field around your seat. You do not make eye contact. You pray that the person next to you doesn't speak, doesn't smell, and doesn't encroach on the demilitarized zone of the armrest. The goal is to survive the journey with your bubble intact.

Trains are different. Trains are dangerous. Not in a physical sense, but in a social one. On a train, the bubble pops.

I learned this on the night train from Budapest to Bucharest.

I had booked a couchette. If you aren't familiar with the terminology, a "couchette" is essentially a rolling hostel room. It has six bunks, three on each side, stacked like shelves in a bakery. It is intimate. You are sleeping inches away from strangers. There is no privacy. There is only the shared reality of the rails.

I boarded at 7:00 PM, dragging my bag, dreading the lottery of roommates. I wanted to be alone. I wanted to read my book, drink the cheap wine I had smuggled on board, and stare out the window in moody silence.

I slid open the door to Cabin 412 and realized my plan was doomed.

The cabin was already occupied by a man who took up approximately 80% of the available volume. He was massive. He had a beard that looked like a bird's nest and was wearing a tracksuit that had seen better decades. He was currently peeling a hard-boiled egg with the focus of a bomb disposal expert.

"Hello!" he boomed. "I am Bogdan. You take top bunk. I take bottom. Is good?"

He didn't wait for an answer. He slapped the vinyl mattress of the top bunk. I nodded, mumbled a thank you, and climbed up, hoping to retreat into my book.

But then, the third roommate arrived. She was a tiny, terrifyingly elegant French woman in her seventies, wearing a silk scarf and carrying a leather handbag that probably cost more than the train itself. She looked at the cramped cabin, looked at Bogdan, looked at me, and let out a sigh that could have deflated a tire.

"Mon dieu," she whispered. "C'est petit."

So there we were. The Setup. A brooding American writer, a Romanian giant, and a Parisian matriarch, trapped in a metal box hurtling through the Carpathian Mountains.

For the first hour, we adhered to the Air Travel Protocol. Silence. Bogdan ate his eggs. The French woman (her name was Elodie) inspected the sheets with suspicion. I pretended to read.

But trains have a way of eroding defenses. It's the rhythm. The *clack-clack-whoosh* of the tracks lulls you into a trance. And then, there is the hunger.

Around 9:00 PM, Bogdan stood up. He reached into a bag that seemed to contain an infinite supply of food. He pulled out a loaf of bread, a block of cheese wrapped in wax paper, and a bottle of unlabeled clear liquid.

He looked at me. He looked at Elodie.

"We eat," he announced. It wasn't a question.

He pulled down the small table between the bunks. He sliced the cheese with a pocket knife that looked illegal in twelve countries. He poured the clear liquid into three plastic cups.

"Palinka," he said. "Home made. My father. It kills the bacteria."

Elodie looked at the plastic cup like it contained nuclear waste. Then, she looked at Bogdan's hopeful, bearded face. She hesitated. And then, the mask cracked. A small, mischievous smile played on her lips. She reached into her expensive handbag and pulled out a box of artisanal dark chocolate.

"For dessert," she said.

I contributed my smuggled wine. And just like that, the treaty was signed.

We ate. We drank the Palinka. It tasted like gasoline and plums and fire. It hit my stomach and exploded. Elodie coughed, her eyes watering, and laughed—a rich, throaty laugh that filled the small cabin.

"My husband," she said, wiping her eyes, "he would hate this. He hated dirt. He hated noise. He traveled only First Class." She took another sip. "He died last year."

The silence that followed wasn't awkward. It was heavy. The train rattled over a switch.

"I am sorry," Bogdan said gently. He poured her a little more fire-water.

"I am not," she said, looking out the black window where the lights of Hungarian villages were streaking by. "He was a boring man. He never let me eat onions. He said it was vulgar." She grabbed a piece of Bogdan's cheese, which definitely contained onions. "I am going to Bucharest to see a lover I haven't seen in forty years. Maybe he is dead too. Maybe he is fat. I don't care. I am going."

I stared at her. This woman, who I had judged as a snob ten minutes ago, was on a rogue mission of romance and rebellion.

Bogdan nodded solemnly. "I go to Bucharest to bury my brother," he said. He raised his cup. "He was not boring. He was crazy. He owe me money. I loved him."

They looked at me. It was my turn. The Confessional was open.

In an airport lounge, I would have made up a story. I would have said I was traveling for work. But here, with the Palinka burning my throat and these two strangers stripping their souls bare, the truth felt like the only option.

"I'm running away," I said. "I quit my job. I broke up with my boyfriend. I don't know who I am anymore. I'm hoping if I keep moving, I'll figure it out."

Bogdan laughed. He reached over and clapped a hand on my shoulder that nearly dislocated it.

"You are young!" he roared. "You are supposed to be lost! If you know who you are at twenty-something, you are boring. Be lost! It is good!"

Elodie nodded. "The lost ones are the interesting ones. My husband knew exactly who he was. He was a dentist. It was terrible."

We talked until 3:00 AM. We talked about love, about death, about the specific grief of losing a sibling, about the terror of starting over. We argued about politics.

We shared the chocolate. The cabin smelled of cheese, alcohol, and sweat, and it was the most comfortable place I had ever been.

There was no Wi-Fi. No notifications. No escape. We were forced to be human beings, interacting in real-time, without the buffer of a screen or a social hierarchy.

I realized then that this is the real "Flex" of train travel. It isn't just about the legroom or the view. It's about the collision.

Air travel is designed to keep us apart, to stratify us by class and status. The curtain between Economy and Business is a wall.

But the train is a mixer. It throws a Romanian construction worker, a Parisian widow, and a lost American writer into a blender and hits "pulse."

By the time we rolled into Bucharest the next morning, we were hungover, tired, and bonded for life.

Bogdan helped Elodie with her bag. She kissed him on both cheeks. She turned to me and grabbed my hand.

"Do not find yourself too quickly, chérie," she said. "The search is the fun part."

I watched them disappear into the crowd on the platform. I never saw them again. I don't know if Elodie found her lover. I don't know if Bogdan buried his brother well.

But standing there in the station, smelling the diesel and the coffee, I didn't feel lonely anymore. I felt part of the stream. I felt the messy, beautiful, chaotic web of humanity that you can only find when you stop flying over the world and start moving through it.

I walked out into the city, gritty-eyed and headachey, and I felt absolutely electric.

This was the journey. The rest was just logistics.

Chapter 8: The "Slowmad" Protocol: Depth Over Breadth

There is a specific kind of exhaustion that only hits you when you are standing in a security line at 5:00 AM on a Tuesday, holding a plastic tray containing your belt, your shoes, and your dignity.

It's the exhaustion of the "Bucket List" traveler.

You know this person. Maybe you *are* this person. They treat the world like a supermarket sweep. They have a checklist of countries that is longer than the Magna Carta. They spend their lives frantically hopping from capital city to capital city, spending exactly 48 hours in each, taking the same photo of the same cathedral, eating the same overpriced "local" meal, and then rushing back to the airport to do it all over again.

They are collecting flags. They are collecting stamps. But they aren't collecting *experiences*.

They are skimming the surface of the planet like a skipping stone. They touch the water, sure. But they never get wet.

This behavior is driven by a very modern, very toxic anxiety: The Fear of Missing Out (FOMO). We have convinced ourselves that if we don't see *everything*, we haven't seen *anything*. We measure the success of a trip by the sheer volume of geography we consumed.

But here is the Manson-style reality check: **Depth beats breadth. Every single time.**

You can learn more about a country by sitting in the same coffee shop for two weeks than you can by visiting five cities in five days. You can understand a culture better by buying groceries in a local market than by taking a guided tour of a palace.

This chapter is about a radical shift in strategy. It is about stopping the frantic hop. It is about planting your feet.

We call it the **"Slowmad" Protocol**.

It is a hybrid of "Slow Travel" and "Digital Nomadism." But you don't need to be a tech bro with a laptop to do it. You just need to be willing to trade the dopamine hit of "newness" for the deep, slow burn of "belonging."

Part I: The Mathematics of Stasis

Why Moving Less Means Living More

Let's look at the "Fastmad" approach—the standard digital nomad or tourist itinerary.

You fly into Barcelona on Friday. You spend Saturday hungover and Sunday sightseeing. Monday you fly to Lisbon. Tuesday you work from a noisy cafe. Wednesday you see a castle. Thursday you fly to Berlin.

What have you actually accomplished?

1. **You are broke.** Short-term accommodation is the most expensive thing you can buy. Last-minute flights are wealth destroyers.
2. **You are exhausted.** Your cortisol levels are permanently spiked because your brain never has time to settle. You are constantly navigating new maps, new languages, and new transit systems.
3. **You are a ghost.** You pass through these cities without leaving a trace or making a connection. You are a blurred figure in the background of someone else's life.

Now, let's look at the **Slowmad** approach.

You fly into Lisbon. You stay for a month.

The Financial ROI:

When you rent an apartment or stay in a guesthouse for 28 days or more, the price drops. On Airbnb or local rental sites, the "monthly discount" is often 30% to 50%.

You aren't buying 30 individual nights; you are buying a block of time.

You aren't taking four flights; you are taking one. That's hundreds of dollars saved (and hundreds of kilos of carbon not emitted).

The Emotional ROI:

This is the big one.

When you stay in one place for a month, you stop being a tourist and start being a resident pro tempore.

You unpack your bag. You actually put your clothes in a drawer. Do you know how good that feels? To hide the suitcase? It's a psychological signal to your brain: We are safe. We are home.

You stop rushing. You don't have to see the castle today because you are here for four weeks. You can see the castle next Tuesday.

Suddenly, the pressure valve releases. You can spend a rainy Tuesday just reading a book or working, without feeling like you are "wasting" your trip.

The Slowmad Protocol isn't about laziness. It's about efficiency. It's about realizing that 4 weekends in 4 cities = 0 understanding. But 4 weeks in 1 city = a lifetime of understanding.

Part II: The "One Base" Rule

The Strategy of the Hub

The core mechanic of this protocol is the **"One Base" Rule**.

The Rule: For every region you visit, you pick **one** headquarters, and you do not move your sleep location for at least 30 days.

If you want to explore Tuscany, you don't stay in Florence, then Siena, then Pisa. You rent a farmhouse outside of Siena for a month, and you do day trips.

If you want to explore Thailand, you don't island hop every two days. You pick Koh Lanta and you stay there.

Why this works:

1. The "Regular" Effect (The Bourdain Factor)

Anthony Bourdain understood this better than anyone. The best travel experiences don't happen on the first visit. They happen on the third, or the fourth, or the tenth.

They happen when the old man at the corner store recognizes you.

They happen when the barista knows you take your coffee black.

They happen when the neighbor stops looking at you with suspicion and starts nodding hello.

You cannot manufacture this. You cannot buy this on Viator. You have to earn it with *time*.

When you are a "regular," the city unlocks itself.

The waiter tells you, "Don't order the fish today, order the special."

The bartender tells you about the festival happening in the next village that isn't on Google Maps.

You stop being a mark. You start being a person.

2. The Productivity Hack

If you are working while traveling (the "Nomad" part of Slowmad), moving constantly is career suicide.

You cannot do deep work if you don't know where the Wi-Fi is or where you are going to sleep tonight.

By establishing a base, you build a routine. You find your "office" (a coworking space or a quiet cafe). You get your work done efficiently so you can actually enjoy your free time, rather than half-working, half-traveling in a state of perpetual panic.

Part III: Community Integration

How to Hack Belonging

So, you've rented the apartment. You've unpacked the bag. Now what?

If you just sit in your room and watch Netflix, you aren't a Slowmad. You're just a hermit in a different time zone.

You need to integrate. You need to build a micro-life.

Here is the tactical guide to hacking belonging in 48 hours.

1. The "Third Place" Strategy

Sociologists talk about the "Third Place."

First Place = Home.

Second Place = Work.

Third Place = The community anchor where you hang out.

In your normal life, this might be your gym, your church, or your pub. When you travel, you need to find a Third Place immediately.

The Gym/Studio:

Join a local gym or yoga studio for a month. Don't buy a day pass. Buy a membership.

Why? Because gyms are one of the few places where locals and expats mix naturally.

You go at the same time every day. You see the same faces. Eventually, you talk.

"Hey, are you using that bench?" turns into "Where are you from?" turns into "Do you want to grab a beer?"

The Coworking Space:

If you work from home, don't. Work from a coworking space.

Yes, it costs money. Pay it.

You aren't paying for a desk; you are paying for instant community. Coworking spaces in places like Lisbon, Bali, or Mexico City are social hubs. They have happy hours. They have WhatsApp groups. They are the fastest way to plug into the local "scene" without being a weirdo at a bar.

2. The Caffeine Anchor

Find one coffee shop.

Not the most famous one. Not the one on the "Top 10" list.

Find a small, locally owned one near your apartment.

Go there every single morning at the same time. Order the same thing. Tip well.

By Day 3, they will recognize you.

By Day 7, they will have your drink ready when you walk in.

By Day 14, you are part of the furniture.

This sounds trivial, but it is psychologically grounding. In a world where everything is foreign, having one place where you are "known" anchors your sanity.

3. The Language Effort

You don't need to be fluent. But you need to try.

Learn the "Big Five":

1. Hello.

2. Please.

3. Thank you.

4. Sorry/Excuse me.

5. The bill, please.

And learn one "Icebreaker."

"The food is delicious." (Oishi desu in Japan, Que rico in Mexico).

When you say this to a waiter or a street vendor, their face changes. You have crossed the line from "Consumer" to "Human."

Part IV: The Ethical Minefield

Don't Be a Colonizer

We need to have a Manson-style "Hard Talk" here.

Digital Nomads are annoying.

In fact, in many cities (Lisbon, Mexico City, Medellin), they are hated.

Why?

Because they are functionally gentrifiers on steroids.

They swoop in with San Francisco salaries, outbid the locals for apartments, drive up the price of coffee, and turn neighborhoods into English-speaking bubbles. They treat the city like a backdrop for their Zoom calls, not a real place with real problems.

This is the "Airbnb Ethics" problem.

When investors buy up entire apartment blocks to turn them into short-term rentals for tourists, families get evicted. The neighborhood loses its soul. The butcher shop becomes a trendy brunch spot that sells $12 avocado toast.

If you are going to be a Slowmad, you have a responsibility to not be a pest. You need to tread lightly.

The Ethical Protocol:

1. Avoid the "Ghost Hotels"

Do not rent apartments that have clearly been bought solely for Airbnb. You can spot them: they look like IKEA showrooms, they have zero personal touches, and the host has 50 other listings.

Instead, look for:

- **"Guest Suites" in someone's home:** You are paying a local family directly.
- **Aparthotels:** These are licensed businesses that are zoned for tourism. They don't displace residents from residential housing.

- **Locally Owned Guesthouses:** This is the gold standard. You get the privacy of a room, but the community of a hotel.

2. Inject Capital Locally (The Leakage Check)

We talked about this in Chapter 1, but it applies double here.

If you stay for a month, you have serious spending power.

Don't spend it all at Starbucks and Uber.

Find the local grocery store. Find the local hardware store.

If you hire a cleaner (which is common in nomad hubs), hire them directly or through a local co-op, not through a predatory app that takes a 40% cut.

3. Read the Room

If you are in a cafe and everyone is speaking Spanish, don't scream into your phone in English on a conference call.

If you are in a conservative neighborhood, put a shirt on.

Don't treat the locals like NPCs (Non-Player Characters) in your video game. They are the protagonists. You are the guest.

Part V: The Narrative Arc of a Slowmad Month

What It Actually Feels Like

To understand why this is worth it, let me walk you through the emotional arc of a 30-day stay.

Week 1: The Honeymoon & The Panic

You arrive. Everything is exciting. The food is new. The streets are pretty.

Then, around Day 4, the panic hits.

"What am I doing here? I don't know anyone. I'm lonely. I miss my friends."

This is the Dip.

The Fastmad traveler never hits the Dip because they leave before it happens. They run away from the loneliness.

You are going to sit in it. You are going to rawdog the loneliness.

Week 2: The Routine

You find the gym. You find the coffee shop. You figure out how the recycling works (which is always weirdly complicated in Europe).

You start to have a rhythm. You work in the morning. You explore in the afternoon.

You stop using Google Maps to get to the grocery store.

Week 3: The Breakthrough

This is the magic week.

You run into someone you met at the gym on the street, and you stop to chat.

You find a "Dupe" restaurant that isn't on TripAdvisor, just because you walked past it three times and it smelled good.

You start to feel a sense of ownership. This is my neighborhood.

Week 4: The Melancholy

You realize you have to leave.

You aren't ready. You feel like you just scratched the surface.

You go to your coffee shop for the last time, and you actually feel sad. You say goodbye to the barista.

When you get on the plane, you aren't exhausted. You are full. You have a deep, rich, complex memory of a place that is now part of you.

Part VI: The "Slowmad" Toolkit

How to Execute

You're sold on the philosophy. Here is the execution checklist.

1. The "Wifi-First" Hierarchy

If you are working, Wi-Fi is oxygen.

Do not trust the Airbnb listing that says "Fast Wi-Fi." They lie.

- **Ask for a Speed Test:** Before you book, ask the host to send a screenshot of a speed test. If they refuse, don't book.

- **The Backup Plan:** Always buy a local SIM card with unlimited data the moment you land. If the fiber goes down, you can hotspot.

2. The Kitchen Audit

You are staying for a month. You cannot eat out three times a day. You will get fat and go broke.

You need to cook.

Check the photos for a real kitchen.

- Does it have more than one burner?
- Does it have a full-sized fridge?
- Does it look like a human being has ever cooked a meal there?
- *Pro Tip:* Pack a small "Kitchen Kit." A good sharp knife (in checked bag), a small bag of spices (salt, pepper, chili flakes), and an AeroPress for coffee. These three things save your life in a mediocre rental.

3. The "Landing Pad" Buffer

Don't book the full month instantly if you are nervous.

Book an Airbnb for 3 days.

Use those 3 days to walk around neighborhoods. Look for "For Rent" signs (which are often cheaper than online).

Visit the coworking spaces.

Then, commit to the month.

Part VII: Case Studies

The Tale of Two Travelers

To hammer this home, let's look at two hypothetical travelers doing "Thailand."

Traveler A: The "Fastmad" (Brendan)

- **Itinerary:** 3 days Bangkok, 3 days Chiang Mai, 3 days Phuket, 2 days Koh Samui.

- **Budget:** Blows $2,000 on flights and ferries. Pays premium nightly rates for hotels ($100/night).
- **Experience:**
    - Gets food poisoning in Bangkok because he ate at a tourist trap.
    - Spends 20 hours in transit (planes, taxis, ferries).
    - Meets 5 people, all other drunk tourists in hostels.
    - Working from hotel beds with bad ergonomics.
    - **Result:** Leaves exhausted, with a hard drive full of photos but zero real memories.

Traveler B: The "Slowmad" (Sarah)

- **Itinerary:** 30 days in Chiang Mai (Nimman area).
- **Budget:** Rents a serviced condo for $500/month. Spends $0 on internal flights.
- **Experience:**
    - Joins a local Muay Thai gym. Trains every morning. Gets in the best shape of her life.
    - Finds a coworking space (Yellow or Punspace). Meets a graphic designer from France and a developer from Kenya. They do dinner every Tuesday.
    - Rents a scooter ($80/month). Explores the mountains on weekends. Finds a waterfall with zero tourists.
    - Learns to cook *Khao Soi* from a cooking class she attends weekly.

- **Result:** Leaves with a new skill, 3 new real friends, and a deep love for Northern Thai culture.

Brendan saw Thailand. Sarah lived in Thailand.

Be Sarah.

Conclusion: The Great Deceleration

The world is speeding up. We are encouraged to consume content in 15-second clips and consume countries in 48-hour bites.

The Slowmad Protocol is a rebellion against this acceleration.

It is a declaration that you are not a consumer of geography. You are a student of it.

It is an admission that you cannot understand the world by looking at it through a bus window. You have to get out of the bus. You have to stop moving.

When you stop moving, the noise fades.

And when the noise fades, you can finally hear the place you are in.

You realize that the "Bucket List" is a scam.

You don't need to see 100 countries before you die.

You need to really, truly see a few of them.

You need to let them change you.

And that takes time.

So, cancel the flight to the next city.

Extend the rental.

Go to the grocery store.

Buy the weird fruit you don't recognize.

Say hello to the neighbor.

You live here now.

Now that we've established how to stay, we need to talk about how to eat.

Because if you stay in a place for a month and you keep eating at the "English Menu" restaurants, you have failed the mission.

We are going to teach you how to hunt for the good stuff.

Turn the page to Chapter 9: Feast Like a Local.

The "Third Place" Breakthrough

The first week of living in a new city doesn't feel like an adventure. It feels like a persistent, low-grade fever.

I had just arrived in Mexico City. I had rented an apartment in La Condesa for a month, committed to the "Slowmad" protocol. On Instagram, Condesa looks like a dream - tree-lined avenues, Art Deco buildings, dogs wearing sweaters. But the reality of dropping yourself into a city of twenty-two million people where you know exactly zero of them is a different beast.

This is the phase of travel that nobody talks about. It is the "Ghost Phase."

For the first six days, I was invisible. I floated through the streets like a specter. I worked from my apartment, which smelled faintly of bleach and other people's choices. I ate tacos alone, scrolling through Twitter to avoid eye contact with happy couples. I spoke to no one except to mutter *"Gracias"* to Uber drivers.

By Friday night, the loneliness hit me like a physical blow. It was visceral. I sat on my couch, listening to the muffled sounds of a party happening next door, and I felt a pathetic, childish urge to pack my bag and go home. I wanted to be somewhere where I wasn't an alien. I wanted to be somewhere where the barista knew my name.

I realized I had two choices.

Choice A: Retreat. Spend the next three weeks watching Netflix, ordering Uber Eats, and treating Mexico City as a backdrop for my depression.

Choice B: Force a connection.

I chose B. I needed a "Third Place."

I walked out of the apartment on Saturday morning with a mission. I walked past the trendy "Nomad" cafes - the ones with the Exposed Brick, the $6 lattes, and the sea of MacBooks. Those places are comfortable, but they are sterile. They are transit zones for people just like me.

I wanted the real thing.

I found it on a corner three blocks away. It was a tiny bakery called *Panadería Rosetta*. Not the famous one with the line around the block. A small, nondescript satellite spot. There were no laptops. There were no influencers taking photos of their croissants. There were just three metal tables on the sidewalk, a counter, and a woman behind the machine who looked like she had absolutely no time for my nonsense.

Her name, I would later learn, was Elena.

Day 1 was excruciating.

I walked up. I stuttered through my order in broken Spanish. "Un café americano, por favor. Y... uh... un rol de guayaba."

Elena looked at me. She didn't smile. She punched the order in. She handed me the coffee.

I sat at the metal table. The chair wobbled. I drank my coffee. I felt like an intruder. I felt like everyone walking by knew I didn't belong there. I finished in ten minutes and fled.

Day 2 was the same.

I ordered. Elena gave me the receipt with the efficiency of a robot. The chair still wobbled. I sat there for fifteen minutes this time, forcing myself to read a book instead of staring at my phone. I felt self-conscious, like an actor on a stage who forgot their lines.

Day 3. The "Dip."

I woke up and thought, Why am I doing this? The coffee at the Airbnb is free.

But the "Slowmad" rules are strict. You have to show up.

I went back.

Elena looked up when I walked in. She didn't smile, but her eyes flickered with recognition.

"Americano?" she asked.

"Sí. Y el rol," I said.

That was it. Two words. But it was a crack in the ice.

By Day 7, the shift began.

I wasn't just "The Gringo" anymore. I was "The Gringo Who Comes at 9:00 AM." I had become a data point in her day. A predictable variable.

I started noticing the rhythm of the street. I saw the same guy walking his Golden Retriever. I saw the old man who sold lottery tickets on the corner. I wasn't just watching the movie anymore; I was an extra in the background scene.

The breakthrough happened on Day 12.

It was raining. A torrential, sudden Mexico City downpour that turns the streets into rivers in seconds.

I ran to the bakery, soaked to the bone. I burst through the door, dripping water on the floor, shaking my umbrella.

The shop was full. Locals were huddled inside, waiting out the storm. There were no tables.

I stood there, awkward and dripping, ready to turn around and leave.

Elena looked up from the espresso machine. She saw me.

She didn't ask for my order. She grabbed a ceramic mug - not the to-go cup I usually got, but a real mug. She pulled an Americano. She put a guava roll on a plate.

Then, she shouted something rapid-fire in Spanish to a guy sitting alone at a small table in the corner.

He looked up, nodded, and kicked out the empty chair opposite him.

Elena pointed at the chair. *"Siéntate,"* she commanded. *Sit.*

I sat.

The guy opposite me was an older man reading a newspaper. He looked at me, looked at my soaking wet shirt, and laughed.

"Mucho agua," he said.

"Mucho," I agreed.

Elena brought the coffee over. She set it down. And then, for the first time in two weeks, she smiled. A real, tired, genuine smile.

"Te vas a enfermar," she said. You're going to get sick.

She dropped a jagged, extra piece of biscotti onto my saucer. Free of charge.

"Cómetelo," she said. Eat it.

I sat there for an hour, drinking the hot coffee, listening to the rain hammer against the glass. The old man showed me a picture of his grandson in the newspaper. We didn't speak the same language, but we communicated in grunts and gestures.

I looked around the room. The smell of baking bread and wet pavement was intoxicating. The noise was loud - conversations bouncing off the tile walls, the hiss of the steam wand, the clatter of cups.

And suddenly, the fever broke.

I wasn't a ghost anymore. I wasn't a tourist passing through. I was a regular. I had a seat at the table.

That piece of biscotti tasted better than any Michelin-star meal I have ever had. It tasted like acceptance.

For the rest of the month, that bakery was my anchor.

When I felt lonely, I went to Elena's.

When I needed to think, I went to Elena's.

I learned that the old man's name was Hector. I learned that Elena hated the reggaeton music the morning shift guy played.

When I finally packed my bags to leave Mexico City on Day 30, the hardest goodbye wasn't the apartment. It was the bakery.

I went in for my last coffee. I told Elena I was leaving. "Me voy hoy."

She stopped wiping the counter. She looked at me for a long second.

"Regresa," she said sternly. Come back.

She handed me a bag with two guava rolls in it. "Para el viaje." For the trip.

I walked away from that bakery feeling a heaviness in my chest that is the hallmark of the Slowmad. It's the pain of leaving a life you just started to build.

But it is a good pain. It means you actually lived there.

You didn't just consume the city. You inhabited it.

You paid your dues, you endured the awkward silence, and you earned your place.

That is the breakthrough.

You realize that belonging isn't something you find; it's something you build, one cup of coffee at a time.

Chapter 9: Feast Like a Local: Avoiding the "Tourist Menu" Markup

There is a specific smell that haunts the main squares of every major European city.

It is not the smell of history, or revolution, or old stone. It is the smell of a deep fryer that hasn't been cleaned since the last financial crisis. It is the smell of stale oil, thawing calamari, and cynicism.

You are standing in the Piazza Navona in Rome, or Las Ramblas in Barcelona, or Leicester Square in London. You are hungry. Your blood sugar is crashing. You look around, and you see them: The Restaurants.

They have prime real estate. They have nice outdoor heaters. And they have a waiter standing outside, holding a laminated menu, smiling at you like a shark that just spotted a wounded seal.

"Hello my friend! You hungry? We have best pizza! We have traditional paella! Come in, free shot!"

He is lying to you.

If you sit down at that table, you are about to commit a crime against your wallet, your stomach, and the culture you flew 4,000 miles to experience. You are about to be served a "Paella" that came out of a plastic bag from a factory in an industrial park, heated up in a microwave. You are about to pay €25 for a "Carbonara" made with cream and cheap bacon instead of eggs and guanciale. You are about to drink a "Sangria" that is essentially sugar-water and box wine with a sad slice of orange floating in it like a drowning victim.

This is the **Tourist Menu Markup**.

It is an industry designed to extract maximum cash for minimum effort from people who don't know any better. It relies on the fact that you are tired, intimidated, and afraid of looking stupid.

But here is the Manson-style truth: **If you eat bad food while traveling, it is your fault.**

We live in the golden age of information. You have a supercomputer in your pocket. There is no excuse for eating garbage.

Food is not just fuel. Food is the fastest, most visceral way to understand a place. It is the culture distilled onto a plate. When you eat the real food—the stuff the locals eat—you are ingesting the history, the geography, and the soul of the destination. When you eat the fake stuff, you are just chewing on a stereotype.

This chapter is your survival guide. We are going to teach you how to spot the traps, how to find the "Dupe" restaurants that serve Michelin-quality food for McDonald's prices, and how to order like a local even if you don't speak the language.

We are going to teach you how to feast.

Part I: The Anatomy of a Trap

The Red Flags of Culinary Disaster

You need to develop a radar. You need to be able to look at a restaurant from fifty yards away and know, instinctively, that it is a crime scene.

Here are the universal rules of the "Do Not Eat" list.

1. The "Picture Menu" Rule

If there are photos of the food on the menu, run.

This is the single most reliable indicator of garbage.

Why? Because good food changes. A real chef goes to the market, sees that the asparagus looks good today, and puts asparagus on the menu. He doesn't have time to take a professional photo of it, laminate it, and stick it on a board outside.

Photos are for fast food. Photos imply standardization. If you see a faded photo of a burger or a plate of pasta that looks a bit too orange, it means the food is mass-produced. It means they are selling you a product, not a meal.

- *The Bourdain Corollary:* If the photos are sun-bleached and look like they were taken in 1993, the food will taste like it has been in the freezer since 1993.

2. The Barker (The "Hello My Friend")

In a good restaurant, the staff is busy. They are busy cooking, serving, and pouring wine. They do not have time to stand on the sidewalk and beg you to come in.

If a restaurant needs to hire a guy to harass pedestrians, it means the food isn't good enough to bring people in on its own.

The Barker is a predator. His job is to spot the weak—the confused family, the couple arguing over Google Maps—and herd them into the pen.

- *The Reaction:* Don't be polite. Don't engage. Keep walking. The moment you make eye contact, you have lost leverage.

3. The "Translation" Spreadsheet

Look at the menu. Is it translated into six different languages? Is there a German column, a Russian column, a Chinese column, and an English column?

This is a bad sign.

A local restaurant writes its menu for locals. It might have a small English translation in the back, or the waiter might help you, but the primary language should be the local one.

If the menu tries to appeal to everyone, it will satisfy no one. It is the culinary equivalent of a "Best of the 80s" compilation CD. It's generic.

4. The Geography Trap

Never eat within a two-block radius of a major tourist attraction.

Do not eat on St. Mark's Square. Do not eat next to the Eiffel Tower. Do not eat overlooking the Acropolis.

You are paying for the view, not the food. The rent in these locations is astronomical. To make a profit, the restaurant must cut costs on ingredients. They are serving you the cheapest possible food at the highest possible price because they know you are paying for the selfie, not the soup.

- *The Dupe Strategy:* Walk three blocks. Just three. Turn down a side street. Turn down another side street. The rent drops. The crowd thins. The food quality triples. The price halves.

Part II: The "Menu Del Dia" Strategy

The Worker's Lunch (The Ultimate Dupe)

If you want to eat like a king on a pauper's budget, you need to understand the rhythm of the city.

In much of the world—especially Europe and Latin America—lunch is the main event. It isn't a sad desk salad eaten in front of a computer screen. It is a ritual.

And for the working class, it is subsidized.

Enter the **Menu del Dia** (Menu of the Day).

This concept was popularized in Spain by Franco (a dictator with a mixed legacy, but he did mandate cheap lunches for workers), but variations of it exist everywhere. In France, it's the *Formule*. In Italy, it's the *Pranzo di Lavoro*.

The Economics:

Restaurants need guaranteed volume. They offer a set menu (usually three courses: starter, main, dessert/coffee, plus wine and bread) for a fixed, incredibly low price.

We are talking €12 to €15 in Spain. €16 to €20 in France.

For that price, you get real food. Homemade lentil soup. Grilled hake with garlic. Flan. A bottle of house wine to share.

How to Find It:

You won't find the Menu del Dia on the laminated English menu they hand to tourists. That menu has the €18 burger.

You look for a chalkboard.

It will be handwritten. It will be leaning against the wall or hanging behind the bar. It will list 3-4 options for "Primero" (First) and "Segundo" (Second).

The Vibe:

Walk into a place at 2:00 PM. Is it loud? Is there a TV playing the news or soccer? are there guys in paint-splattered overalls or office workers with loosened ties eating there?

This is the jackpot.

These people eat here every day. If the food was bad, the place would close. If the price was too high, the place would close.

This is the ultimate market validation.

The Bourdain Angle:

There is a specific beauty to the worker's lunch. It is unpretentious. The wine comes in a glass carafe, not a bottle with a fancy label. The bread is plonked on the tablecloth (no plate). The service is fast and efficient, not fawning.

You are eating the fuel that powers the city. You are breaking bread with the people who build the roads and file the taxes. It is a communion of the mundane, and it is delicious.

Part III: The Market Hack

Chaos, Freshness, and the "Standing Room Only" Rule

If you really want to understand a culture, skip the museum and go to the wet market.

Museums are where cultures store their dead things. Markets are where they keep their living things.

The market is the beating heart of the food system. It is loud. It smells of raw meat, brine, spices, and sawdust. It is visually overwhelming. And it is the best place to eat in the entire city.

The Strategy:

Most great markets (La Boqueria in Barcelona, Mercado Central in Santiago, Tsukiji Outer Market in Tokyo) have food stalls or small counters nestled among the vendors.

These places have zero "food miles." The chef literally walks ten feet to the fishmonger, buys a fish, walks back, and throws it on the grill.

You cannot get fresher than that.

The Rules of Market Eating:

1. The "Standing Room" Indicator

Look for the stall with no chairs. Look for the counter where people are standing, elbow-to-elbow, eating clams or tacos or noodles.

If people are willing to stand up to eat the food, the food is worth it. Comfort is secondary to flavor.

If a place has empty tables and comfortable chairs in the middle of a busy market, ask yourself why.

2. Follow the Grandmas

This is a universal law of travel. If you see a queue of elderly local women waiting for a specific food stall, get in that queue immediately.

Grandmas have two things:

1. Decades of cooking experience (they know what good food is).

2. No patience for bullshit.

They will not wait in line for mediocre food. If they are waiting, whatever is at the end of that line is the truth.

3. The "One Thing" Rule

The best stalls often sell only one thing.

A place that sells only Porchetta sandwiches. A place that sells only Pho. A place that sells only Empanadas.

Specialization breeds perfection. If a guy has spent 20 years making nothing but grilled chicken, he is going to make the best damn grilled chicken you have ever tasted.

Avoid the stall that sells pizza, sushi, and burgers. That is a factory of disappointment.

Specific Market Dupes:

- **Barcelona:** Everyone goes to **La Boqueria**. It's great, but it's a zoo.
    - *The Dupe:* Go to **Mercat de Santa Caterina**. It's ten minutes away. It has a colorful wavy roof. It is full of locals. The food counters serve incredible seafood for half the price of Boqueria.
- **London:** Everyone goes to **Borough Market**. It's beautiful, but you can't move.
    - *The Dupe:* Go to **Maltby Street Market**. It's tucked into railway arches nearby. It's gritty, cool, and the food is insane.
- **Tokyo:** Everyone tries to go to the new Toyosu market (sterile).
    - *The Dupe:* Go to the **Tsukiji Outer Market** streets. Eat the Tamagoyaki (egg omelet) on a stick. Eat the uni (sea urchin) straight out of the shell. It's chaotic and perfect.

Part IV: The Zero-Kilometer Diet

Eating Local to Save the World (and Your Palate)

Let's pivot to the "Conscious Maya" side of things. We need to talk about carbon.

Food production accounts for a massive chunk of global emissions. But a huge percentage of that isn't the growing of the food; it's the **transport** of the food.

We have broken the seasons.

We expect to eat strawberries in December. We expect to eat avocados in Scotland. We expect to eat Atlantic salmon in the middle of the desert.

To make this happen, we wrap food in plastic, put it on airplanes, and fly it thousands of miles. This is insanity.

The "Food Miles" Reality:

- An asparagus spear flown from Peru to London has a carbon footprint roughly 20 times higher than one grown in the UK.
- Eating "local" is often more effective at reducing your carbon footprint than being vegetarian but eating imported goods.

The Zero-Kilometer Philosophy:

The "Dupe Hunter" eats what is close.

When you are in Italy, you don't order the burger. The beef probably came from somewhere else. You order the pasta with truffles found in the hills nearby.

When you are in Thailand, you don't order the wine (which is imported and taxed 300%). You drink the beer or the rum.

When you are on an island, you eat the fish.

Why this tastes better:

This isn't just about being a "good eco-citizen." It's about flavor.

An avocado that ripened on the tree in Mexico tastes like butter and sunshine. An avocado that was picked rock-hard in Mexico, gassed in a warehouse, and shipped to a hotel in Iceland tastes like wet play-doh.

Food that has traveled is tired. Food that is local is alive.

The "In Season" Challenge:

Before you travel, do one Google search: "What is in season in [Destination] in [Month]?"

- **Italy in October:** Porcini mushrooms, truffles, pumpkins.

- **Japan in April:** Bamboo shoots, strawberries, sea bream.
- Mexico in August: Chiles en Nogada (a specific seasonal dish).

If you order these things, you are getting the best ingredients at the cheapest price (abundance lowers cost). You are eating in sync with the planet.

Part V: Street Food Safety

How to Be adventurous Without the ER Visit

One of the biggest fears travelers have—especially the "David" persona—is getting sick. "Montezuma's Revenge." "Delhi Belly."

This fear drives people into the arms of the Tourist Traps. They think the sterile-looking hotel restaurant is safer than the street cart.

This is a lie.

I have gotten food poisoning from hotel buffets more often than from street stalls. Why? Because in a buffet, the food sits out for hours, lukewarm, breeding bacteria.

At a good street stall, the food is cooked fresh, right in front of your face, at high heat. Fire kills bacteria.

The Street Food Safety Protocol:

1. The "High Turnover" Rule

You want the busy stall. You want the stall where the cook can't make the food fast enough.

High turnover means the ingredients aren't sitting around. The meat goes from the cooler to the grill to your mouth in minutes.

Never eat at the empty stall with the sad pile of pre-cooked meat stacked up in the corner. That is a bacteria condo.

2. Watch the Hands

Look at the cook. Is he handling the money and the food with the same bare hand?

That's a no-go.

Ideally, one person cooks, and another person handles the cash. Or, the cook uses a glove/tongs for the food.

3. "Boil It, Peel It, or Forget It"

This is the classic rule for raw ingredients in developing countries.

- **Fruit:** If you can peel it (banana, orange, mango), it's safe. The skin protects the fruit. If you eat the skin (apple, grapes) and it's been washed in tap water, it's a risk.
- **Salad:** Avoid salad in places where the water isn't drinkable. Lettuce is washed in tap water. It is the number one cause of stomach issues for travelers. Skip the lettuce; eat the cooked veggies.
- **Ice:** In most tourist hubs (even in SE Asia/Mexico), ice is now made in factories with purified water. It's usually fine. But if you see a guy chipping a block of ice with a rusty pick on the sidewalk? Maybe skip that one.

4. The Morning Rule

Eat street food when the market opens (morning/lunch). The ingredients are fresh.

By 9:00 PM, that raw chicken might have been sitting in the sun for 12 hours. Risk increases as the day goes on.

Part VI: The Alcohol Strategy

Drink What the Locals Drink

Tourism marketing has convinced us that a vacation requires fancy cocktails with umbrellas.

But in most cultures, the locals aren't drinking Mai Tais.

The Wine Trap:

In the US, "House Wine" is a euphemism for "the cheapest vinegar we could find."

In Europe (Italy, France, Spain, Portugal), House Wine (Vino della Casa) is usually excellent. It is locally produced, young, and meant to be drunk with food.

It is also dirt cheap.

You can get a liter carafe for €8.

Don't be the guy scanning the wine list for a recognizable Label like "Pinot Grigio." Just ask for "Rosso" (Red) or "Bianco" (White).

You will be drinking what the locals drink. It will pair perfectly with the food. And you won't wake up with a sulfite-induced headache (mostly).

The "Aperitivo" Hack:

In Italy, there is a holy hour called Aperitivo (usually 6pm-8pm).

You buy a drink (a Spritz or a Negroni) for €8.

And suddenly, a magical buffet appears. Chips, olives, little sandwiches, pasta salad, focaccia. It is free. It is included with the drink.

You can effectively have a light dinner for the price of one cocktail.

It is the most civilized tradition on earth.

- *The Trap:* Going to dinner at 6:30 PM. The restaurants are empty (Italians eat at 9 PM).

- *The Dupe:* Go to Aperitivo at 7 PM. Soak up the vibe. Then go to dinner late, like a pro.

Part VII: How to Order (When You Don't Speak the Lingo)

The "Point and Smile" Method

The fear of the language barrier keeps people in the Tourist Trap. They want the English menu because it feels safe.

But you are a Hunter. You want the real stuff.

Here is how to survive a local restaurant with zero language skills.

1. Google Lens

This is your magic wand. Open the Google App on your phone. Click the camera icon. Point it at the chalkboard menu.

It will translate the text in real-time overlaid on your screen.

It's not perfect (it might translate "Pollo a la Brasa" as "Chicken to the Coal"), but it gives you the gist.

2. The "Oishi" Technique (The Neighbor Method)

Look around the room. What looks good?

See a guy eating a soup that looks amazing?

Catch the waiter's eye. Point discreetly at the guy's soup. Smile. Nod.

This is a universal language. It says: "I want what he is having."

Locals love this. It shows you trust their taste.

3. Ask "What is Good?"

Don't ask "What do you recommend?" (They might recommend the most expensive thing).

Ask "What is typical?" or "What is fresh?"

- Spanish: *¿Qué me recomienda?*
- Italian: *Cosa mi consiglia?*
- French: Qu'est-ce que vous me conseillez?

If the waiter hesitates and then points to a dish, order it. Even if you don't know what it is.

This is the adventure.

Maybe it's tripe. Maybe it's squid ink. Maybe it's the best thing you'll ever eat.

Worst case scenario? You hate it. You're out €12. You buy a slice of pizza later.

But you tried.

Part VIII: The Narrative: The Best Meal of My Life

A Case Study in Simplicity

I want to end this chapter with a story, to prove a point.

A few years ago, I was in Vietnam, in the Mekong Delta. I was on a small boat, miles from any "TripAdvisor Recommended" establishment. We pulled up to a rickety wooden dock attached to a shack on stilts.

There was no menu. There were no walls. There was just an old woman with a charcoal brazier and a cooler.

She didn't speak English. I didn't speak Vietnamese.

She pointed to the cooler. I nodded.

She pulled out a river prawn the size of my forearm. It was blue and alien-looking.

She threw it on the grill. No marinade. No sauce. Just fire and shell.

Five minutes later, she handed it to me on a plastic plate with a small bowl of salt, pepper, and lime juice.

I peeled it, burning my fingers. I dipped the white meat into the lime-pepper sludge.

It was explosive. It was sweet, smoky, salty, and sharp. It tasted like the river. It tasted like the jungle.

I sat on a plastic stool, watching the brown water of the Mekong flow by, eating this prawn with my bare hands, juice running down my arm.

It cost $2.

That meal ruined me. It ruined me for every white-tablecloth, foam-garnished, $100 shrimp dish I have had since. Because I realized that luxury isn't about the thread count of the napkin or the number of waiters hovering over you.

Luxury is proximity to the source.

Luxury is the skill of an old woman who has grilled a million prawns.

Luxury is the absence of bullshit.

The "Tourist Trap" sells you a simulation of this experience. They sell you a frozen prawn in a themed restaurant with bamboo on the walls to make it look like the Mekong.

The "Dupe Hunter" goes to the actual Mekong.

You have a choice. You can eat the simulation, or you can eat the reality.

The reality is cheaper. The reality is messier.

But the reality nourishes you in a way the simulation never will.

Part IX: The "Feast Like a Local" Checklist

Your Pocket Guide

Before you walk out the door to find dinner, run this mental checklist.

1. **The Visual Scan:**
    - No photos on the menu?
    - No barker outside?
    - Menu in local language (mostly)?
    - Busy with locals (or grandmas)?
2. **The "Menu del Dia" Check:**
    - Is it lunch time (1pm - 3pm)?
    - Is there a chalkboard?
    - Is the price under €15/$15?
3. **The "Zero-Kilometer" Audit:**
    - Am I ordering something that grows/lives nearby?
    - Is it in season?

4. **The Fear Factor:**
   - Does this place look a little intimidating?
   - Is the lighting harsh?
   - Are the napkins paper?
   - *Good.* You are in the right place.

Conclusion: The Final Bite

Eating well while traveling is an act of respect.

It is respect for the farmers who grew the food.

It is respect for the culture that invented the recipes.

And it is respect for yourself.

You worked hard to earn the money for this trip. Don't waste it on mediocrity.

Don't be the person who flies to Italy and eats at the Hard Rock Cafe.

Be the person who is elbow-deep in a bowl of clams at a market stall, trying to ask the guy next to you for a napkin in sign language, laughing because the food is so good it makes you want to cry.

That is the feast we are hunting for.

Now, wipe your mouth. We have packed the bag, ridden the train, found the hotel, and eaten the food.

But we need to talk about what goes in the bag.

We need to talk about the gear. Because looking like a sustainable traveler is half the battle (and packing light is the other half).

Turn the page to Chapter 10: The Ethical Gear Guide.

Chapter 10: The Ethical Gear Guide: Aesthetic Minimalism

Let's talk about the cargo pants.

You know the ones. They have seventeen pockets. They unzip at the knee to become shorts, a transformation that has never, in the history of human fashion, looked good on anyone. They are made of a synthetic material that makes a "swish-swish" sound when you walk, announcing your virginity to everyone within a three-block radius.

For some reason, when we decide to go traveling, we lose our minds. We abandon our personal style and dress like we are going on a safari in 1996. We buy "travel clothes" that are designed to be "practical," but actually just signal to the entire world: *"Please rob me, I am a tourist and I have traveler's checks in my hidden money belt."*

This is the opposite of the Dupe Hunter aesthetic.

If you want to travel sustainably, you don't need to dress like a park ranger, and you definitely don't need to dress like a hippie wrapped in a burlap sack.

True sustainability is **Aesthetic Minimalism**.

It is the art of owning less, but owning *better*. It is the realization that you are dragging your insecurities around behind you in that 50-pound suitcase. You pack too much because you are afraid. You are afraid of the rain. You are afraid of a fancy dinner. You are afraid of being cold. So you pack for every hypothetical "What If" scenario, and you end up burdened, sweaty, and miserable.

The Dupe Hunter travels light. We travel with **One Bag**. We move through airports like ghosts, bypassing the check-in counter and the baggage claim. We hop on trains without dislocating our shoulders. We look good enough to walk into a Michelin-starred restaurant, but our gear is tough enough to hike a volcano.

This chapter is your permission slip to stop packing like a hoarder and start packing like a pro.

Part I: The Philosophy of the Carry-On

The Baggage is Metaphorical

Here is a hard truth: **If you can't carry it for a mile without stopping, you have too much stuff.**

When you check a bag, you are surrendering your freedom. You are tethering yourself to the airline's incompetence. You are the person standing at the carousel in Rome, watching empty rubber flaps spin around for forty-five minutes, praying that your underwear didn't end up in Helsinki.

Checking a bag is a "Tourist" move.

Carry-on only is a "Traveler" move.

But beyond the logistics, there is the Ethical Argument.

Consumerism is the engine of climate change. We buy cheap crap, we use it three times, it breaks, we throw it away, and it sits in a landfill for ten thousand years.

The fashion industry is one of the biggest polluters on the planet. "Fast Fashion" (H&M, Zara, Shein) is built on a model of planned obsolescence and exploitation.

When you travel with a massive suitcase, you are usually filling it with fast fashion. You are treating clothes as disposable.

The One-Bag Philosophy forces you to opt out of that cycle.

When you only have 35 liters of space (about the size of a standard backpack), you can't afford to pack garbage. Every item has to earn its rent. Every item has to be durable, versatile, and high-quality.

You stop buying "more" and you start buying "better." You move from a "Consumer" mindset to a "Custodian" mindset. You buy a shirt that will last you ten years, not ten weeks.

This is the Vimes' Boots Theory of economics: The rich stay rich because they can afford to buy things that last, while the poor stay poor because they have to keep replacing cheap things.

Travel gear is the same. Spending $80 on a merino wool t-shirt hurts. But spending $10 on a cotton t-shirt that smells like death after one wear and has holes in it after three washes hurts more in the long run.

Part II: The Fabric Revolution

Why Cotton is the Enemy

If you take one thing away from this chapter, let it be this: **Cotton is a traitor.**

Cotton is comfortable when you are sitting on your couch. But the moment you start moving, sweating, or traveling, cotton tries to kill you. It absorbs moisture like a sponge. It holds onto bacteria (which creates the smell). It takes three days to dry.

If you are "Rawdogging" a flight or hiking in Albania, and you are wearing a cotton t-shirt, you will be damp, cold, and smelly within four hours.

You need the magic fabric. You need **Merino Wool**.

The Merino Miracle

I know what you're thinking. "Wool? In the summer? Are you insane?"

You are thinking of the scratchy sweater your grandma knitted you. That is traditional wool.

Merino is different. It comes from a specific breed of sheep (mostly in New Zealand) that live in extreme environments. Their wool fibers are microscopic. They are soft, not scratchy.

Here is why Merino is the G.O.A.T. (Greatest of All Textiles) for the Dupe Hunter:

1. The "5 Wears, 1 Wash" Rule

Merino wool is naturally antimicrobial. The fibers contain lanolin and have a structure that prevents bacteria from latching on.

Bacteria = Smell.

If bacteria can't breed, the clothes don't smell.

You can wear a merino t-shirt for five days in a row - hiking, sweating, sleeping in it - and at the end of the week, it will smell like... nothing.

This is the secret to packing light. You don't need 7 shirts for a 7-day trip. You need 2.

You wear one, you pack one. Boom. You just saved 50% of your luggage space.

2. Temperature Regulation

Sheep don't have air conditioning. Their wool has evolved to keep them cool in the summer and warm in the winter.

Merino does the same for you. It wicks moisture away from your skin before it turns into sweat vapor. It is a personal climate control system.

A thin merino layer works in 90°F (32°C) heat and 40°F (4°C) chill. This means you don't need a "summer wardrobe" and a "winter wardrobe." You just need layers.

3. The Aesthetic

Merino looks expensive. It has a matte finish. It drapes well.

A black merino t-shirt looks like a t-shirt at the gym, but it looks like a "fashion top" under a blazer at dinner. It is the ultimate shapeshifter.

The Ethical Caveat

Merino is an animal product. You must buy Mulesing-Free wool. (Mulesing is a cruel practice involving cutting skin off sheep). Look for brands like Icebreaker, Smartwool, or Unbound Merino that certify their wool is ethical.

If you are strictly vegan, look for Tencel or Hemp. They aren't quite as magical as Merino, but they are miles better than cotton or polyester.

Part III: The "Eco-Gear" That Actually Looks Good

Aesthetic Minimalism

The goal is to avoid the "Backpacker" look.

The Backpacker looks like they are about to climb Everest, even if they are just going to a museum. They wear neon colors. They have zippers everywhere. They look technical.

The Dupe Hunter adopts the Gray Man Theory.

This is a security concept used by spies and special forces. The goal is to blend in. To look unremarkable. To not draw attention.

If you look like a local (or a expat working in the city), you are less likely to be scammed, pickpocketed, or overcharged.

The Capsule Wardrobe Strategy

A capsule wardrobe is a small collection of clothes that all match each other.

- **The Palette:** Stick to neutrals. Black, charcoal, navy, olive, white.
    - *Why:* If every shirt matches every pair of pants, you can get 30 outfits out of 8 items. If you bring a bright Hawaiian shirt, it only matches one pair of shorts. That is inefficient.
- **The Silhouette:** Slim but not tight. Tailored but comfortable.
- **The Vibe:** "Aesthetic Minimalism." Clean lines. No logos. No slogans.

The Gear Breakdown:

1. The Pants

You need one pair of pants that can do everything.

Look for "Technical Chinos." Brands like Outlier, Western Rise, or Lululemon (the ABC pant) make pants that look like dress slacks but stretch like yoga pants.

You can hike up a mountain in them, brush off the dust, and wear them to a Michelin-star dinner. They dry in 20 minutes in a hotel sink.

- *Quantity:* 1 worn, 1 packed (optional).

2. The Layers

Instead of a heavy coat, pack layers.

- **Base:** Merino T-shirt.
- **Mid:** A Merino hoodie or a cashmere sweater.
- **Outer:** A lightweight rain shell (Patagonia or Arc'teryx).
- *The Puff:* A "Packable Down Jacket" (Uniqlo makes a cheap one, Patagonia makes an ethical one). It scrunches down to the size of a grapefruit but keeps you warm in freezing temps.

3. The Shoes (The Impossible Choice)

Shoes are the heaviest thing you pack.

Ideally, you bring one pair.

I know. It sounds impossible. But hear me out.

You need a shoe that is comfortable enough to walk 20,000 steps in, but stylish enough not to look like a gym shoe.

- *The Solution:* The "Heritage Boot" or the "Minimalist Sneaker."
    - **Blundstones:** The traveler's cult favorite. They are slip-on boots. They are waterproof. They are indestructible. They look good with jeans. You can hike in them. You can go to dinner in them.
    - **White Leather Sneakers:** (Common Projects, Koio, or Vejas). They go with everything. They look crisp. But they are terrible for hiking.
- *The Compromise:* Wear the heavy boots/shoes on the plane. Pack a pair of super-lightweight sandals (Bedrock or Luna) or a pair of collapsible loafers.

Part IV: The Toiletries Revolution

Solids, Bars, and the End of Spills

Here is a scenario that has happened to everyone: You open your suitcase after a long flight. You smell peppermint. You look inside. Your bottle of Dr. Bronner's has exploded. Your clothes are covered in soap. You want to scream.

Liquids are the enemy of the One-Bag traveler.

1. They explode.
2. They are heavy (water weighs 1kg per liter).
3. The TSA hates them. You have to put them in the little baggy. You have to take them out. It's a humiliation.

The solution is the **Solid Revolution**.

1. Shampoo Bars

This isn't a bar of soap. It is high-quality shampoo, dehydrated into a puck.

- **The Win:** One bar lasts as long as three bottles of liquid shampoo.
- **The Plastic Win:** No plastic bottle to throw away. Zero waste.
- **The TSA Win:** It's a solid. It stays in your bag. No security theater.
- *Brand:* **Ethique** or **Lush**. (Ethique is better - zero plastic packaging).

2. Solid Toothpaste (Tabs)

Little tablets that look like mints. You chew them, wet your toothbrush, and brush.

- **The Win:** No messy tube. You can count exactly how many you need (14 days = 28 tabs). Precise packing.
- **The Brand: Bite** or **Humble Co**.

3. Deodorant Paste/Bar

Ditch the aerosol (bad for ozone, bulky). Ditch the plastic roll-on.

Get a concentrated paste in a tin or a cardboard tube.

- **The Win:** Lasts forever. Smells like essential oils, not "Arctic Blast" chemicals.

4. The Safety Razor

Disposable plastic razors are an environmental crime. They are unrecyclable trash.

Get a metal Safety Razor.

- **The Win:** The blades cost 10 cents. The shave is better. The handle lasts a lifetime.

- *Caveat:* You can't take the *blades* in carry-on. You have to pack the handle (empty) and buy a pack of blades when you land (available at any pharmacy in the world). It's a fun little mission for your first day.

Part V: The Water Strategy

Defeating the Plastic Bottle Lobby

We mentioned this in the Tropical chapter, but we need to get into the specs.

Buying water in plastic bottles is the ultimate "Tourist Tax." You are paying a 2,000% markup for something that flows out of the ground.

And in places like Asia or South America, where you can't drink the tap water, tourists feel like they have no choice.

You have a choice.

You need a Water Filter Bottle.

There are two main players in this game: **LifeStraw** and **Grayl**.

Option A: The Filter (LifeStraw / Brita)

This removes flavor, chlorine, and some bacteria.

- *Good for:* Europe, USA, cities where the water is safe but tastes like pool water.

- *Not good for:* India, Mexico, rural Thailand. It won't stop viruses.

Option B: The Purifier (Grayl Geopress)

This is the nuclear option.

It looks like a French Press. You fill it with nasty water (from a hotel tap in Delhi, or a creek in Peru). You press it down.

In 8 seconds, it physically removes viruses, bacteria, protozoa, and heavy metals.

- **The Win:** You have safe drinking water *anywhere*.
- **The Math:** A Grayl costs ~$90. A bottle of water costs $2. If you drink 3 bottles a day, the Grayl pays for itself in 15 days.
- **The Planet Win:** You save ~300 plastic bottles per trip. That is a mountain of plastic you didn't create.

The "Vibe" Check:

Carrying a massive Nalgene bottle makes you look like a college student.

The Grayl or a sleek stainless steel bottle (like a Klean Kanteen) looks professional. It sits on a dinner table without looking out of place.

Part VI: The Tech Setup

Digital Nomad Minimalism

If you are a "Slowmad," you need your office. But you don't need Best Buy in your backpack.

1. The Universal Adapter

Don't bring five different plugs. Get one GaN (Gallium Nitride) Universal Adapter.

- *The Tech:* GaN technology makes chargers smaller and cooler. A generic adapter is the size of a brick. A GaN adapter is the size of a golf ball but can charge a laptop.

- *The Flex:* Get one with 3 USB-C ports. You can charge your laptop, phone, and watch simultaneously from one outlet. This is crucial when you are in a hostel or a cafe with only one plug.

2. The Cables

Bring high-quality braided cables. They don't tangle.

- *The Hack:* Bring a 6-foot (2-meter) cable. Why? Because hotel outlets are never where you need them. They are behind the bed or across the room. A long cable gives you freedom.

3. The Power Bank

Essential. Your phone is your ticket, your map, and your wallet. If it dies, you are stranded.

Get a 10,000mAh bank. It's the sweet spot between weight and power (charges an iPhone 3 times).

- *Brand:* **Anker** or **Nitecore** (Nitecore makes ultralight carbon fiber ones for hikers).

4. The Noise Management

We talked about "Silent Travel." But sometimes you can't escape the noise.

You need AirPods Pro or equivalent noise-canceling earbuds.

They are tiny. They block out the screaming baby on the plane. They create a bubble of sanity.

Part VII: The Bag Itself

The One Ring to Rule Them All

You have the gear. Now, what do you put it in?

Do not - I repeat, do not - bring a top-loading hiking backpack.

You know the ones. They are tall and skinny. They have a drawstring at the top.

If you need the socks at the bottom, you have to dump the entire contents of the bag onto the floor of the airport. You look like a hobo explosion.

You need a Clamshell Travel Backpack.
It opens like a suitcase (flat), but carries like a backpack.
The Specs:

- **Size:** 35 Liters to 40 Liters. This is the maximum "Carry-On" size for most airlines.
- **Material:** Ballistic Nylon or X-Pac (sailcloth). Waterproof and tear-proof.
- **Aesthetic:** Black. Matte. Minimal branding. No dangling straps.
    - *Why:* You want to be able to walk into a 5-star hotel lobby without looking like you just crawled out of the woods. You want to be able to carry it into a business meeting if necessary.

The Top Contenders:

- **Peak Design Travel Backpack:** The photographer's favorite. Beautiful, functional, expensive.
- **Aer Travel Pack 3:** The digital nomad favorite. Organization for days. Sleek city look.
- **Cotopaxi Allpa:** The "Fun" option. Opens like a butterfly. Colorful (maybe too colorful for the Gray Man look, but very functional).
- **Osprey Farpoint 40:** The budget king. Not the prettiest, but indestructible and comfortable.

Part VIII: The "One-Bag" Packing List Checklist

The 7kg Challenge

Here is the Manson-style challenge. Most budget airlines (Ryanair, AirAsia) have a 7kg (15lb) weight limit for carry-on.

If you go over, they force you to check it and charge you $50.
The Dupe Hunter never pays the fee.
Here is the **Visual Guide to Packing Under 7kg**.

Worn on Plane (The Bulky Stuff):

- 1x Pants (Chinos/Jeans)
- 1x Merino T-Shirt
- 1x Mid-layer (Sweater/Hoodie)
- 1x Shoes (Boots/Sneakers)
- 1x Jacket (Shell)

Packed in Bag (The Payload):

- **Clothes Cube:**
  - 3x Merino T-Shirts (Black, Navy, Grey)
  - 1x Shorts (Hybrid - can swim in them or wear to gym)
  - 4x Underwear (Merino or ExOfficio synthetic)
  - 4x Socks (Merino wool - Darn Tough brand)
  - 1x Button-down shirt (Linen or Merino - for nice dinners)
- **Tech Pouch:**
  - Universal GaN Adapter
  - Cables (USB-C, Lightning)
  - Power Bank

    - Headphones
- **Dopp Kit (Solids):**
    - Shampoo Bar
    - Deodorant
    - Toothpaste Tabs + Brush
    - Safety Razor handle
    - Moisturizer (small tin)
- **Misc:**
    - Water Filter Bottle (Empty)
    - Sunglasses
    - Pen + Notebook (Sensory Log)
    - Passport
    - Microfiber Towel (if staying in hostels/camping)

Total Weight: ~6.5kg.

The Feeling:

Imagine walking off the plane. You bypass the baggage claim crowd - those sad souls staring at the conveyor belt. You walk straight out the door.

You hop on the local bus. Your bag sits on your lap.

You arrive at your hotel. You unzip one zipper. You are unpacked.

This is freedom.

You are not a beast of burden. You are a traveler.

Part IX: Laundry: The Hobo Bath for Clothes

The Secret to "Packing Less"

The only way the 7kg list works is if you do laundry.

But you aren't going to a laundromat every three days. That's a waste of time.

You are going to do the **Sink Wash**.

The Technique:

1. **The Bag:** Bring a **Dry Bag** (like a Scrubba) or just use the hotel sink.
2. **The Soap:** Use a slice of your shampoo bar or a Dr. Bronner's solid bar.
3. **The Agitation:** Put clothes in sink/bag. Add water and soap. Knead like dough for 2 minutes. Let soak for 10 minutes.
4. **The Rinse:** Rinse until no bubbles.
5. **The Burrito Method:** This is the pro tip.
    - Lay a dry towel on the bed.
    - Lay your wet t-shirt flat on the towel.
    - Roll the towel up tight like a burrito with the shirt inside.
    - Twist it. Stomp on it. The towel sucks 90% of the water out of the shirt.
6. **The Hang:** Hang the shirt on a chair or a travel clothesline.
    - Because it is Merino or tech fabric, it will be bone dry in the morning.

Total time: 10 minutes.

Cost: $0.

Result: Infinite clean clothes.

Part X: The "Buy It For Life" (BIFL) Mindset

Investing in Your Freedom

I can hear the "Conservation David" persona asking: *"But isn't all this expensive?"*

Yes.

A Merino shirt is $80. A Grayl bottle is $90. A Peak Design bag is $300.

The total kit might cost $800.

But let's look at the math of **Cost Per Use**.

Scenario A: The Cheap Tourist

- Buys a $50 suitcase (wheels break after 3 trips).
- Buys 5 cotton t-shirts for $10 each ($50). They shrink and smell.
- Buys travel-sized toiletries every trip ($15).
- Buys water bottles at the airport ($5 each).
- Checks a bag ($50 each way).

Over 5 years of travel, the Cheap Tourist spends thousands on fees, replacements, and disposable items.

Scenario B: The Dupe Hunter

- Buys the $300 bag. It has a lifetime warranty. If it breaks, they fix it. It lasts 20 years.
- Buys the $80 Merino shirt. wears it 200 times. Cost per wear: $0.40.
- Buys the Filter Bottle. Never buys water again. Saves $200 per trip.

- Never checks a bag. Saves $100 per trip.

The "Expensive" gear pays for itself in two trips.

After that, it is pure profit.

This is the definition of Ethical Consumption. You are supporting companies that build things to last. You are rejecting the "landfill economy."

You are buying gear that respects your intelligence and respects the planet.

Conclusion: The Dignity of Efficiency

There is a quiet dignity to having your shit together.

When you are the person who breezes through security because you don't have liquids to fish out...

When you are the person who isn't sweating through their shirt because they are wearing wool...

When you are the person who doesn't need to hunt for a convenience store because you have a water filter...

You feel competent.

Travel is chaotic. Trains are delayed. Hotels get overbooked. It rains.

You cannot control the world.

But you can control your gear.

Your pack is your shell. It is your home.

Keep it light. Keep it clean. Keep it ethical.

And for the love of god, burn the zip-off cargo pants.

Now that you are packed, prepped, and fed, we need to address the elephant in the room. Or rather, the elephant you are trying to ride.

We need to talk about Wildlife.

Why "hugging a sloth" is the ultimate red flag, and how to see animals without being a monster.

Chapter 11: Wildlife & Welfare: Don't Be That Person

There is a photo that exists on the dating profiles of approximately 40% of the human population.

You know the one. The guy is wearing a Bintang singlet and cargo shorts. He is squatting in the dust, grinning like he just won the lottery. And next to him, with a heavy chain around its neck and eyes that look like they are staring into a void of existential despair, is a full-grown tiger.

The guy thinks this photo says: *"I am adventurous. I am an apex predator. I am one with nature."*

What this photo actually says is: *"I gave twenty dollars to a roadside zoo to drug a wild animal so I could get three likes on Tinder."*

It is the ultimate "Ick".

It is the moment where tourism stops being about curiosity and starts being about domination. It is the moment we decide that a living, breathing, sentient creature exists solely to be a prop in the movie of our lives.

We need to have a hard conversation about animals.

Because here is the truth: We love animals. We are obsessed with them. We watch *Planet Earth*. We cry when the dog dies in the movie. We fly halfway around the world specifically to see the exotic creatures that we read about in storybooks.

But that love? It is often toxic. In our desperate need to get close, to touch, to "bond," we are fueling an industry of cruelty that is so dark, so cynical, and so profitable that it would make a cartel boss blush.

We are going to talk about the difference between **Wildlife** and **Wallet-life**. We are going to learn the rules of engagement. And we are going to learn why the most ethical thing you can do for an animal is to stay the hell away from it.

Part I: The Disneyfication of Nature

The "Snow White" Complex

We have been conditioned by cartoons.

Since we were children, we have been fed a steady diet of movies where the animals talk, sing, and desperately want to be our friends. We think that if we go into the jungle, the monkeys will want to shake our hands and the birds will land on our shoulders.

We suffer from **Main Character Syndrome**. We believe that nature is a stage set for our amusement.

When a tourist sees a wild animal, their first instinct is often: "How can I get closer?"

Their second instinct is: "How can I get a photo of ME with IT?"

This is where the industry steps in. They know you want the "Snow White" moment. They know you want the selfie. So, they manufacture it.

But nature—real nature—is not a petting zoo. Nature is indifferent to you.

A real tiger does not want to take a selfie with you. A real tiger wants to eat you, or avoid you, or mate, or sleep. It definitely does not want to have a stranger's arm draped over its neck.

To make the animal comply with your fantasy, the animal has to be broken.

The "Ick": Why It's Cringe (and Cruel)

Let's break down the "Big Three" of animal tourism traps. These are the activities that seem harmless or even "educational" on the surface, but are actually nightmares in disguise.

1. The Tiger Selfie

The Fantasy: You are bonding with a majestic beast. It's calm because it senses your good vibes.

The Reality: It's calm because it is stoned out of its mind.

Most "Tiger Temples" or "Photo Parks" use a cocktail of sedatives to keep the animals docile. They are often declawed. Their teeth are filed down. They are taken from their mothers at birth so they imprint on humans, a process that involves starvation and beatings to ensure submission.

When you pay for that photo, you are funding a prison. You are paying for the drugs.

And honestly? It looks stupid. Everyone knows it's fake. It's like taking a photo with a cardboard cutout, except the cutout has a beating heart and trauma.

2. The Elephant Ride

The Fantasy: You are a Maharaja. You are trekking through the jungle on the back of a gentle giant. It's symbiotic.

The Reality: The Phajaan (The Crush).

This is the hardest thing to read in this book, but you need to know it.

An elephant is a wild animal. It is huge, powerful, and independent. It does not naturally allow a human to ride on its spine (which, by the way, is the weakest part of its anatomy and prone to collapse under the weight of a howdah chair).

To get an elephant to accept a rider, it must be "crushed."

This happens when they are babies. They are tied up in a small cage. They are beaten with bullhooks (metal spikes). They are starved. They are kept awake for days.

The goal is to break their spirit. To terrify them so deeply that they will obey any command to avoid the pain.

Every time you see a tourist swaying on top of an elephant, you are seeing the result of torture. That elephant isn't "tame." It is suffering from complex PTSD.

3. The Dolphin Swim

The Fantasy: Flipper! They are smiling! They love jumping!

The Reality: The Smile is a lie.

Dolphins possess an anatomical quirk: their jaw is shaped in a permanent upward curve. We interpret this as a smile. They "smile" when they are happy. They "smile" when they are dead.

In captivity, dolphins are kept in chlorinated tanks that blind them. They rely on echolocation (sonar) to see. In a concrete tank, their sonar bounces off the walls, creating a maddening cacophony. It drives them insane.

Swimming with them creates immense stress. They are often on anti-depressants (yes, really) to keep them from ramming the walls.

This is the "Ick."

Once you know the truth, you can't unsee it. You look at those vacation photos and you don't see joy. You see exploitation. You see a transaction where the animal pays everything, and the tourist pays $50.

Part II: The Golden Rule

If You Can Hug It, It's Drugged

We need a heuristic. A simple rule to navigate the confusing world of animal tourism.

Here it is. Memorize it.

"If you can hug it, it's drugged."

Or broken. Or restrained. Or dying.

Wild animals do not hug humans. They do not want to be hugged.

- If you can pet the tiger... **Run.**
- If you can ride the elephant... **Run.**
- If the monkey is wearing a diaper... **Run.**
- If the sloth is hanging passively on a handler's arm in broad daylight... **Run.** (Sloths are nocturnal and solitary; being passed around a crowd causes them heart failure).

There is **zero** scenario where a truly wild, healthy animal will allow a stranger to touch it.

The Corollary: The "Selfie" Distance

If you are close enough to take a selfie with a wild animal (meaning it is within arm's reach behind you), you are too close.

Ethical wildlife photography requires a telephoto lens (zoom). It requires distance.

If you are using the front-facing camera, you are the problem.

Part III: The "Sanctuary" Scam

How to Detect Greenwashing in the Jungle

The industry is smart. They know that "Zoology" is out and "Sustainability" is in.

So, they changed the signs.

"Bob's Roadside Zoo" became "The Bob Foundation for Wildlife Rescue."

"Elephant Rides" became "Elephant Bathing Experiences."

They greenwashed the cages.

This is the **Sanctuary Scam**. Millions of well-meaning travelers (like you) get duped every year. They think they are volunteering or supporting a rescue center, but they are actually funding a breeding mill.

Here is how to spot the "Eco-Lie".

1. The "No Breeding" Rule

A real sanctuary does not breed animals. Period.

The goal of a sanctuary is to provide a home for animals that cannot be released (due to injury or habituation). They do not want more animals in cages.

If you see baby animals everywhere—baby tigers, baby monkeys, baby elephants—it is not a sanctuary. It is a farm.

They are breeding them because babies are cute and babies sell tickets. But babies grow up. And when a tiger gets too big to be cuddled, what happens to it? (See: Canned Hunting, below).

2. The "Interaction" Red Flag

Does the "Sanctuary" offer you the chance to handle the animals?

- "Walk with Lions!"
- "Bathe the Elephants!"
- "Hold a baby Orangutan!"

A real sanctuary minimizes human contact. The goal is to keep the animals as wild as possible.

If the business model relies on you touching the merchandise, it's a scam.

3. The "Canned Hunting" Connection

This is the darkest secret in Africa.

You go to a "Lion Sanctuary" in South Africa. You pay to bottle-feed a cub. It's adorable. You feel like you are helping.

You are told the cub was "abandoned" (a lie; it was stripped from its mother).

When that cub gets too big to cuddle, it is moved to the "Lion Walk" experience.

When it gets too dangerous for that, it is sold to a hunting ranch.

A rich tourist pays $50,000 to shoot a lion. The lion is released into a fenced enclosure. It is often drugged. It has no fear of humans because you bottle-fed it.

The hunter shoots it. He poses for a photo.

This is the lifecycle of the "Lion Cub Selfie." From the bottle to the bullet.

Part IV: The Dupe Strategy

The Switch: Captivity vs. The Wild

So, what do we do? Do we just stop seeing animals?

No.

We switch the venue. We stop going to the animal's prison, and we go to the animal's house.

This is **The Dupe**.

The difference between seeing an animal in captivity and seeing one in the wild is the difference between looking at a prisoner and looking at a king.

In a zoo, the animal is stripped of its context. It is bored. It is diminished.

In the wild, the animal is in charge. You are the guest. You are the one who is small.

1. The Safari Swap

- **The Trap:** The Zoo or the "Safari Park" where animals are in pens.
- **The Dupe:** A real Safari.
    - **Where:** Kruger National Park (South Africa), Masai Mara (Kenya), Udawalawe (Sri Lanka).
    - The Experience: You sit in a jeep. You wait. You smell the dust.

And then, you see it. An elephant emerges from the bush. It is huge. It ignores you. It tears a branch off a tree with a cracking sound that vibrates in your chest.

You hold your breath.

You realize that this animal could flip your car if it wanted to. But it doesn't. It allows you to exist.

That feeling? That mix of fear and awe? That is the drug we are chasing. That is respect.

2. The Marine Swap

- **The Trap:** SeaWorld or "Swimming with Dolphins" in a pool.
- **The Dupe:** Wild Whale/Dolphin Watching.
    - **Where:** The Azores (Portugal), Baja California (Mexico), Vancouver Island (Canada).
    - The Experience: You are on a boat in the open ocean. It is choppy. You might get seasick.

Then, a spout. A Humpback whale breaches. Forty tons of biology launching itself into the air.

It is chaotic. It is unpredictable. You can't control the angle.

But when it happens, it feels like a miracle. You aren't forcing the animal to perform; you are witnessing it live.

3. The Primate Swap

- **The Trap:** The "Monkey Forest" where macaques are aggressive and steal your sunglasses, or the photo-prop chimp.
- **The Dupe:** Gorilla Trekking or Gibbon Spotting.
    - **Where:** Rwanda/Uganda (Gorillas), Borneo (Orangutans).
    - The Experience: You hike for hours through thick mud. You are exhausted. You smell like sweat.

And then you find them. A silverback gorilla eating bamboo. He looks at you with eyes that are undeniably human. He is intelligent. He is calm.

You are allowed one hour. You stay 7 meters away. You wear a mask to protect him from your diseases.

It costs money (permits are expensive), but that money pays for the rangers who protect the gorillas from poachers. Your tourism literally keeps them alive.

Part V: The New Rules of Engagement

How to Be a Ghost

The goal of the Dupe Hunter is to be a ghost in the woods. To see without being seen. To leave no trace.

Here is your operational protocol for wildlife encounters.

1. The "Binocular" Flex

We talked about gear. Here is the most underrated piece of kit: Binoculars.

If you try to watch wildlife with your naked eye or your iPhone, you will be disappointed. You will try to get closer.

Buy a decent pair of binoculars (8x42 is the sweet spot).

Suddenly, you have a superpower. You can see the whiskers on a seal from 100 yards away. You can see the color of a bird's eye.

You get the intimacy of the close-up without the violation of the physical space.

- *The Brag:* "I don't need to get close. I have glass."

2. The Silence Discipline

When you are in the wild, shut up.

We are a noisy species. We talk, we laugh, we step on twigs.

Animals hear everything.

If you want to see the good stuff, you have to practice "Predator Silence." Walk softly. Communicate with hand signals. Stop moving.

The moment you stop moving, the forest comes alive. The birds return. The lizard comes out of the rock.

You have to earn the sighting with your patience.

3. Geotagging is Snitching

This is a new rule for the digital age.

Do not geotag specific locations of endangered animals.

If you see a Rhino in a specific valley in South Africa, do not post the photo on Instagram with the location tag "Hluhluwe-Imfolozi Park, Sector 4."

Poachers use Instagram.

They search for tags. They use your "cool photo" to hunt the animal.

Tag the country. Or the region. Keep the specific location vague. Gatekeep the animals to save them.

Part VI: The Narrative: The Bear in the Berries

A Story of Irrelevance

To understand why "Wild" is better than "Tame," let me tell you about a bear I met in Canada.

I was hiking alone (dumb, I know). I came around a bend in the trail, and there he was. A black bear.

He was about thirty feet away. He was sitting on his haunches, raking huckleberries into his mouth with huge, curved claws.

In a zoo, a bear is a tragedy. It paces. Its coat is dull. It looks at you, waiting for a marshmallow.

This bear glistens. His fur was like obsidian. He was rippling with muscle.

I froze. My heart hammered against my ribs like a trapped bird. I reached for my bear spray.

The bear stopped eating. He lifted his head. He sniffed the air. He looked directly at me.

In that moment, the entire hierarchy of my life dissolved. My credit score, my deadlines, my ego- none of it mattered. I was just meat. I was a slow, soft biped in his living room.

He looked at me for three seconds. He decided I wasn't a threat, and I wasn't food. I was irrelevant.

He grunted, turned his back to me, and went back to the berries.

I backed away, slowly, until I was out of sight. Then I walked for a mile, shaking with adrenaline.

That moment was worth more than a thousand zoo visits.

It wasn't "cute." It was existential.

I felt the weight of his presence. I felt the reality of the food chain. I felt lucky to be alive.

That is what we are looking for. We aren't looking for a pet. We are looking for a reminder that we share this planet with other nations—nations of fur and feather and fin—who do not work for us.

Part VII: The Welfare Check

A Quick Audit Before You Book

Before you book any animal experience—even one that calls itself a "Sanctuary"- run the **Welfare Check.**

1. The Freedom Test:

Does the animal have the freedom to leave?

- *Yes:* It's wild (e.g., a safari, whale watching). **Green Light.**
- *No:* It's captivity. Proceed to Question 2.

2. The Contact Test:

Are you allowed to touch it?

- *Yes:* **Red Flag.** (Unless it's a domesticated animal like a horse or dog).
- *No:* **Green Light.**

3. The Performance Test:

Is the animal doing a trick? (Painting, dancing, jumping through hoops).

- *Yes:* **Red Flag.** Animals don't ride bicycles in nature. This requires abusive training.
- *No:* It is doing natural behaviors (sleeping, eating, grooming). **Green Light.**

4. The Origins Test:

Where did the animals come from?

- *Wild Caught:* **Red Flag.** (Dolphins are often captured from the wild).
- *Rescued:* **Green Light.** (But verify the rescue story).

Part VIII: The Redemption

From Consumer to Steward

We have been hard on you in this chapter. But there is a path to redemption.

If you have taken the tiger selfie in the past? Forgive yourself. You didn't know. The industry is designed to trick you.

But now you know.

The transition from "Tourist" to "Dupe Hunter" is about shifting your money from exploitation to conservation.

1. Buy the Permit

Gorilla trekking permits in Rwanda cost $1,500.

That is a lot of money.

But that money doesn't go to a CEO. It goes to the community. It builds schools. It pays the rangers who risk their lives to stop poachers.

Because of tourism, the Mountain Gorilla population is increasing.

Your money purchased their survival. That is the ultimate flex.

2. Visit the "Boring" Sanctuary

Go to the sanctuary where the animals are far away. Where you have to use your binoculars. Where you might not even see them because they are sleeping in the tall grass.

Support the places that prioritize the animal's welfare over your entertainment.

Write a review: "Didn't see the tiger close up. It was great. 5 Stars."

Normalize the idea that animals deserve privacy.

3. Adopt, Don't Shop (The Souvenir)

Don't buy the ivory carving. Don't buy the tortoise shell bracelet. Don't buy the "kopi luwak" coffee (which comes from caged civet cats).

Instead, "adopt" an animal.

Many legitimate conservation groups allow you to digitally adopt a shark, a turtle, or an elephant. You get updates on its migration. You get a certificate.

It's a better souvenir than a dead piece of animal parts.

Conclusion: Don't Be That Guy or Girl

Let's go back to the dating profile photo. The guy with the tiger.

When you see that photo now, I want you to see the sadness in it. I want you to see the desperation of a person who needs to steal the power of a wild animal because they don't have enough of their own.

Don't be that guy. Be the person who goes to the jungle and sits quietly. Be the person who watches the monkeys from a respectful distance and laughs at their antics without trying to feed them a Cheeto.

Be the person who understands that the magic of the wild is not that it belongs to you, but that it doesn't.

The world is not a petting zoo. It is a wilderness. Keep it wild.

We have covered the animals. We have covered the gear. We have covered the food.

But eventually, the trip has to end. You have to go home.

And that is the hardest part. The "Post-Travel Blues."

How do you integrate what you've learned? How do you keep the "Hunter Mindset" when you are back in the office?

And how do you calculate the damage you did?

Chapter 12: The Return: Reintegration & Redemption

The worst part of travel isn't the turbulence. It isn't the food poisoning. It isn't the guy in seat 14B who takes his shoes off and uses the armrest as a pedicure station.

The worst part of travel is the key in the door.

It's that specific, hollow click when you unlock your apartment after two weeks away. You walk in. The air smells stale. It smells like dead plants and unopened mail. You drop your bag in the hallway, and the sound echoes because the house feels strangely empty, even though all your stuff is there.

You open the fridge. There is a jar of mustard, a shriveled lemon, and a carton of milk that expired three days ago.

You stand there, exhausted, unwashed, and vibrating with the residual energy of a thousand miles, and the silence hits you like a physical blow.

The adventure is over. The movie has ended. The credits are rolling, and now you have to go back to being "You."

This is the Post-Travel Blues

It is a legitimate psychological crash. You have spent weeks running on high-octane dopamine. You have been waking up every day with a mission: *Find the train. Find the food. Survive the hike.* You have been living in high definition.

And now? Now you have to do laundry. Now you have to answer the email from Steve in Accounting about the spreadsheet. Now you have to reintegrate into a life that suddenly feels two sizes too small for the person you have become.

Most people handle this poorly. They get depressed. They scroll through their camera roll, posting "Take me back" photos on Instagram, living in a state of pathetic nostalgia. They treat their "real life" as a waiting room for their next vacation.

But the Dupe Hunter doesn't do that.

The Dupe Hunter understands that the return isn't the end of the trip. It is the final, most crucial phase of the mission. It is the **Reintegration**.

If you only feel alive when you are 5,000 miles from home, you don't have a travel habit; you have a drug problem. The goal isn't to escape your life; the goal is to bring the fire back with you and burn the house down (metaphorically).

In this final chapter, we are going to talk about how to keep the "Explorer Mindset" alive in the suburbs. We are going to calculate the damage we did to the planet. And we are going to talk about **Redemption** - how to pay your debts to the places that changed you.

Part I: The Hangover

Why Normalcy Feels Like a Trap

Let's dissect why the return hurts so much.

When you are traveling - especially the way we have taught you to travel in this book - you are forced to be present. You are navigating the "Rawdog" flight. You are hunting for the "Dupe" restaurant. You are deciphering a train schedule in a language you don't speak.

Your brain is fully engaged. You are problem-solving. You are a hunter-gatherer in a strange land.

When you come home, you switch to autopilot. You know the route to work. You know what the coffee tastes like. You know what your friends are going to say before they say it.

The friction is gone. And without friction, there is no spark.

This is why you feel bored. You aren't bored because your city is boring. You are bored because *you* have stopped looking at it. You have stopped hunting.

You have reverted to being a tourist in your own life - gliding through the days, consuming the same routine, waiting for the weekend.

The Explorer Mindset at Home

So, how do we fix it? How do we keep the high going without booking another flight?

You apply the **Dupe Hunter Protocol** to your own zip code.

Think about it. When you were in Hanoi, you happily sat on a plastic stool in an alleyway to eat soup because it felt "authentic." But at home, you go to the same three chain restaurants because it's "convenient."

When you were in Berlin, you took the train to a weird neighborhood just to look at the graffiti. At home, you haven't been to the other side of town in six years.

You have to treat your hometown as if you have never been there.

The Action Step: The Domestic Safari

This weekend, I want you to do something uncomfortable.

Go to a neighborhood you usually avoid. Go to the immigrant enclave. Go to the "Little Vietnam" or "Little Ethiopia" of your city.

Don't use Yelp. Just walk.

Look for the place with the bad lighting and the line out the door.

Order the thing on the menu you can't pronounce.

You will find that the thrill of discovery isn't geographically bound. It is a mindset.

There are "Dupes" in your city right now. There are hidden gems, weird subcultures, and incredible food that you are ignoring because you think you know this place.

You don't.

Re-learn it.

Part II: The Carbon Ledger

The Bill Comes Due

Okay, the honeymoon is over. We need to look at the receipt.

throughout this book, we have talked about "slashing your footprint." We took the train. We ate the local veggies. We stayed in the eco-lodge.

We did good.

But we still traveled. And travel, by definition, consumes resources.

If you flew, you burned kerosene. If you stayed in a hotel, you used electricity. If you ate, you consumed agriculture.

You have a debt.

Most travel books skip this part. They want you to feel good. They want to sell you the fantasy that "eco-tourism" is zero-impact.

It isn't.

Unless you walked to your destination and ate only berries you foraged yourself, you left a mark.

It is time to open **The Carbon Ledger**.

This isn't about guilt. Guilt is useless. Guilt is just a vanity metric for your ego.

This is about accounting. It's about taking responsibility for the space you occupy.

The Calculation:

I want you to calculate the footprint of your trip.

You don't need a degree in atmospheric science. Use a free calculator like MyClimate or Atmosfair.

Plug in the data:

- **Flights:** (e.g., JFK to LHR, Economy).
- **Accommodation:** (e.g., 7 nights, 3-star hotel).
- **Transport:** (e.g., 500km by train).

The calculator will spit out a number. Let's say it's **1.2 tons of CO2**.

Look at that number. Don't look away.

That is your exhaust. That is the weight of the sky you used up to have your adventure.

Now, the question is: What are you going to do about it?

Part III: Redemption

The Scam of "Offsetting"

The traditional answer is "Carbon Offsetting."

You check a box on the airline website, pay $12, and they promise to plant some trees in the Amazon to suck up your carbon.

I'm going to be honest with you: **Most of that is bullshit.**

The carbon offset market is the Wild West. It is rife with scams, double-counting, and "phantom credits."

Often, the trees they "plant" are monoculture plantations that die in three years, or they burn down in a wildfire (releasing the carbon right back into the air). Or, they protect a forest that wasn't in danger of being cut down anyway.

Buying a cheap offset is like cheating on your spouse and then buying them a gas station bouquet of flowers. It doesn't fix the problem; it just makes *you* feel like you did something.

We need a better strategy. We need **Insetting**.

Insetting vs. Offsetting

In the corporate world, "Insetting" means reducing emissions within your own supply chain.

For the Dupe Hunter, "Insetting" means investing directly in the destination you visited6.

Don't send your money to a faceless "Climate Fund" in Switzerland.

Send your money back to the place that gave you the joy.

The Logic:

Your flight emitted carbon globally. But your presence consumed resources locally.

The best way to balance the scales is to strengthen the community you visited, making them more resilient to climate change and over-tourism.

How to Inset:

Instead of paying $20 to an airline offset program, take $100 (or whatever you can afford) and donate it to a hyper-local NGO in the destination.

- **Did you hike in Nepal?** Donate to the **Himalayan Stove Project** (which provides clean-burning stoves to families, saving forests and lungs).
- **Did you swim in the Caribbean?** Donate to a local **Coral Restoration Foundation**.
- **Did you see wildlife in Africa?** Donate to the specific **Anti-Poaching Unit** of the park you visited.

Why this works:

1. **Efficiency:** The money goes straight to the ground. No middlemen.
2. **Connection:** You are maintaining a relationship with the place. You aren't just a consumer anymore; you are a stakeholder.
3. **Reality:** You can see the impact. You can read their newsletter. You know where the money went.

This is **Redemption**. It is acknowledging that you took something from the place (an experience), and now you are putting something back (resources).

Part IV: Digital Altruism

The Power of the Review

There is one more currency you have, and it is more valuable than Bitcoin.

It is your Review.

We live in an algorithmic dictatorship. Small, sustainable, locally-owned businesses live and die by the algorithm.

The "Tourist Trap" restaurant has 5,000 reviews because they have a marketing budget and a guy on the street harassing people.

The "Dupe" restaurant - the grandma making the best soup of your life - has 12 reviews.

Your job is to balance the scales. This is **Digital Altruism**.

The Protocol:

When you get home, sit down for one hour.

Open Google Maps or TripAdvisor.

Write detailed, glowing reviews for the specific businesses that did it right.

- The guesthouse that didn't wrap the soap in plastic.
- The tour guide who respected the wildlife distance rules.
- The restaurant that served local, seasonal food.

How to write a "Hunter" Review:

Don't just write "Good food, yum." That helps nobody.

Write for the algorithm and the future traveler.

- *"This place is a hidden gem. The owner, Maria, sources all ingredients from within 20 miles. It is the definition of sustainable dining. The price is fair, and the flavor destroys the tourist places on the main square."*

The Gatekeeping Paradox:

I know what you are thinking. "But wait, didn't you say to keep the secrets? If I review it, won't it become a Trap?"

This is the nuance.

- **Gatekeep the Wilderness:** Do not geotag the rhino. Do not geotag the hidden waterfall that can't handle crowds.
- **Share the Economy:** *Do* tag the ethical business.

Small businesses need volume to survive. If the ethical eco-lodge goes bankrupt, a chain hotel will buy the land.

By sending traffic to the "Good Guys," you are voting with your keyboard. You are ensuring that sustainable tourism is profitable.

Part V: The Legacy of the Hunter

You Are Contagious

Here is the final truth about travel: **You never really come back.**

The person who left is not the person who returned.

You have seen the "Paros Peace." You have felt the silence of the "Rawdog" flight. You have tasted the prawn on the Mekong.

You know too much now.

You know that the "Tourist Trap" is a lie. You know that luxury is cheap if you know where to look.

You have a responsibility to be contagious.

When your friends start planning their trips, don't be the annoying "Travel Snob." Don't preach.

Just show them the way.

When they say, "We're thinking of going to Santorini," you say, "That sounds cool. But have you looked at Paros? It's half the price and the food is better. Here, let me show you this place I found."

You are the node in the network. You are the virus of good taste and ethical choices.

If you can convert three people from "Tourists" to "Hunters," you have done more for the planet than a lifetime of recycling soda cans.

The Final Entry

Go to the last page of your Carbon Ledger8.

Write down one promise to yourself.

Not a big, saving-the-world promise. A small one.

"I will not buy water in plastic bottles next year."

"I will take the train if the trip is under 5 hours."

"I will go back."

Close the book.

Unlock the door.

Go inside.

Unpack the bag.

You're home.

But you're not the same.

And that is the point.

Conclusion: The Manifesto of the Dupe Hunter

We started this journey with a panic attack in Santorini. We ended it with a donation to a school in Nepal and a glowing review for a taco stand.

We moved from the **"Trap" to the "Dupe."**

We moved from **"Consumption" to "Connection."**

We moved from **"Guilt" to "Action."**

Travel is a privilege. It is an unfair, carbon-heavy, beautiful, destructive, life-affirming privilege.

We cannot stop doing it. The human urge to see what is over the next hill is too strong.

But we can do it better.

We can stop being the locusts that devour the world, and start being the bees that pollinate it. We can spread wealth. We can support culture. We can bear witness to the wild without taming it.

You have the tools now. You have the apps, the gear, the mindset, and the map.

The world is huge. It is waiting for you.

And it is full of secrets.

Go find them.

www.ingramcontent.com/pod-product-compliance
Lightning Source LLC
LaVergne TN
LVHW012102160826
845678LV00014B/2902

* 9 7 8 1 9 6 3 1 4 2 2 9 7 *